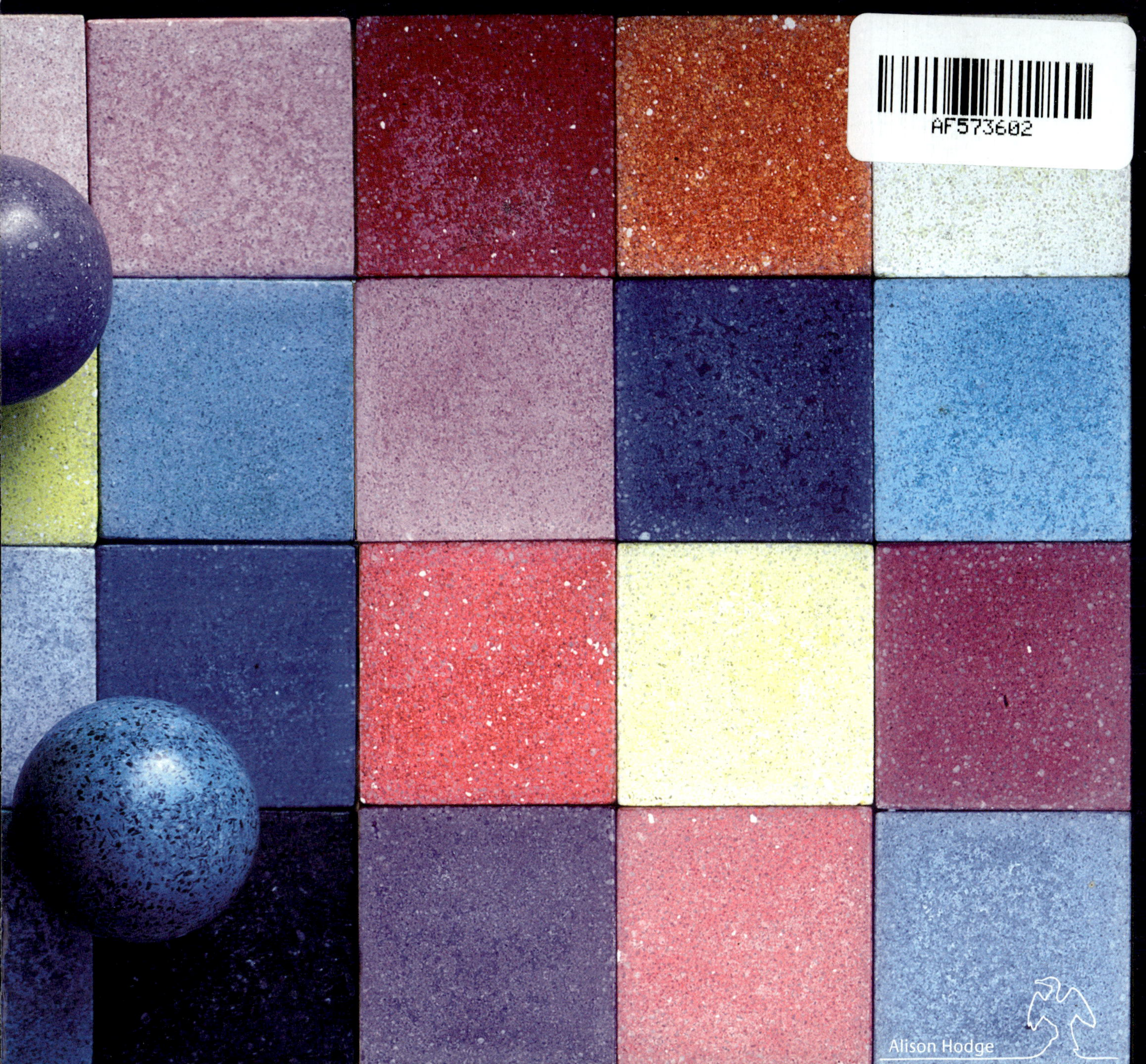
Alison Hodge

concrete works

featuring the work of

CAROLE VINCENT

with photographs by

CLIVE BOURSNELL

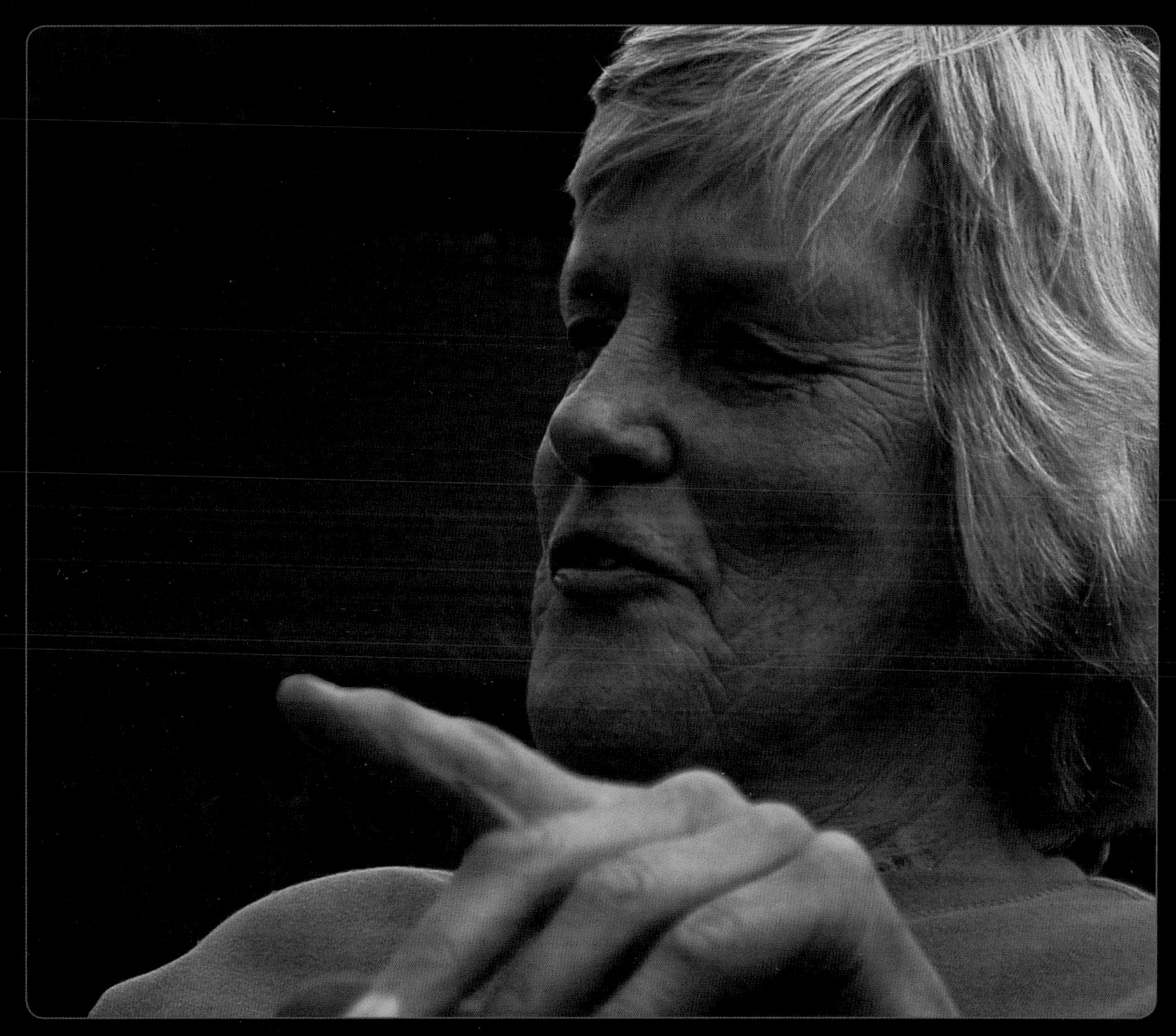

contents

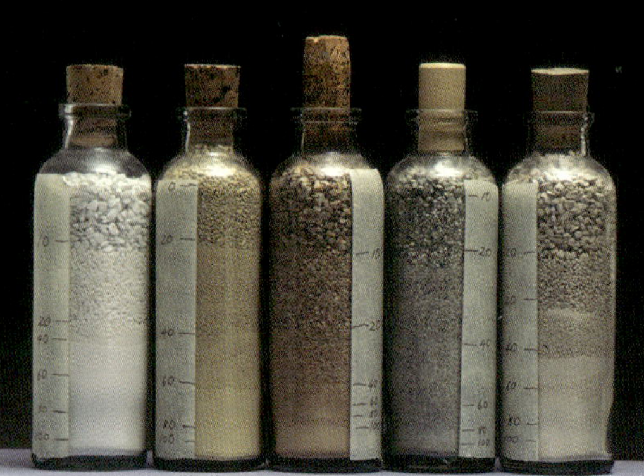

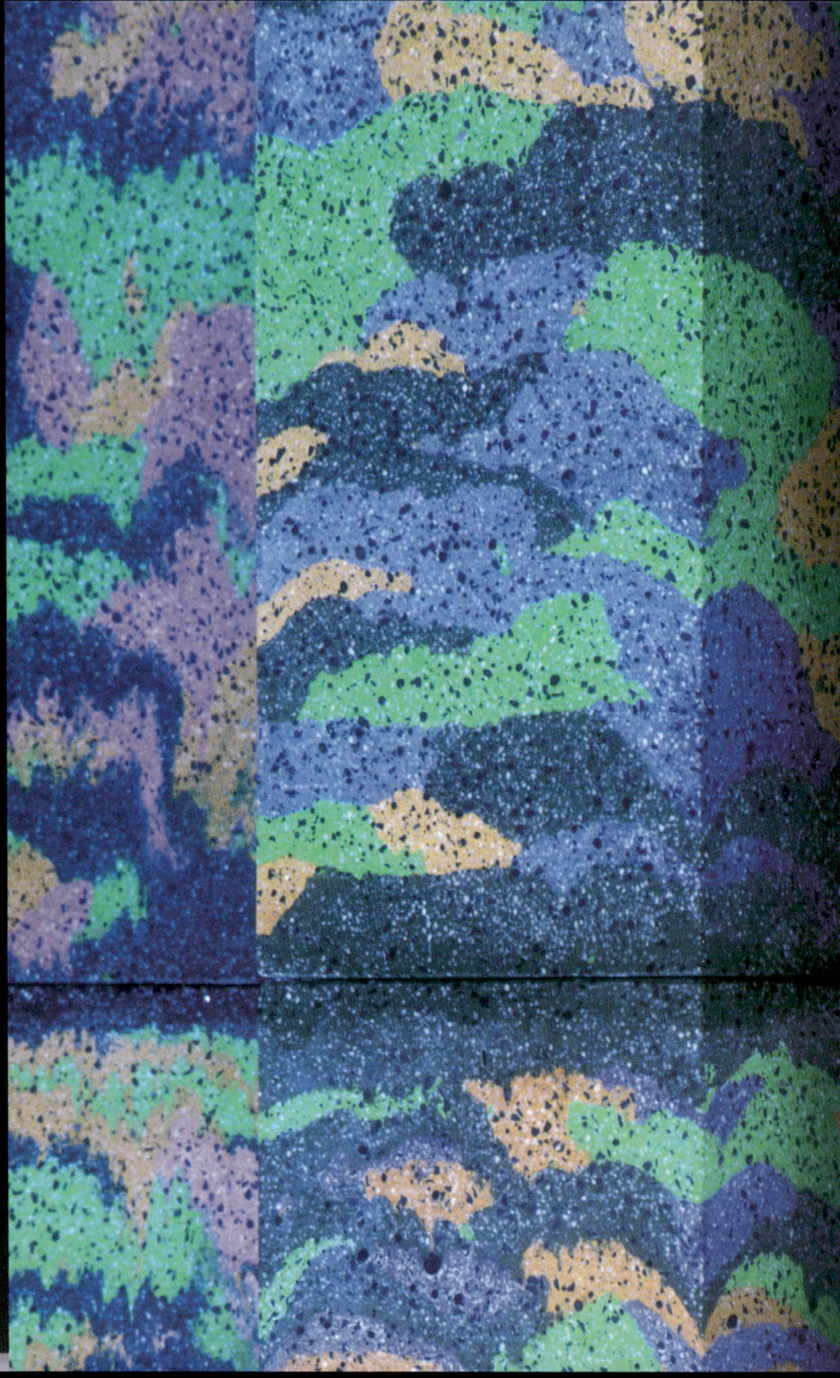

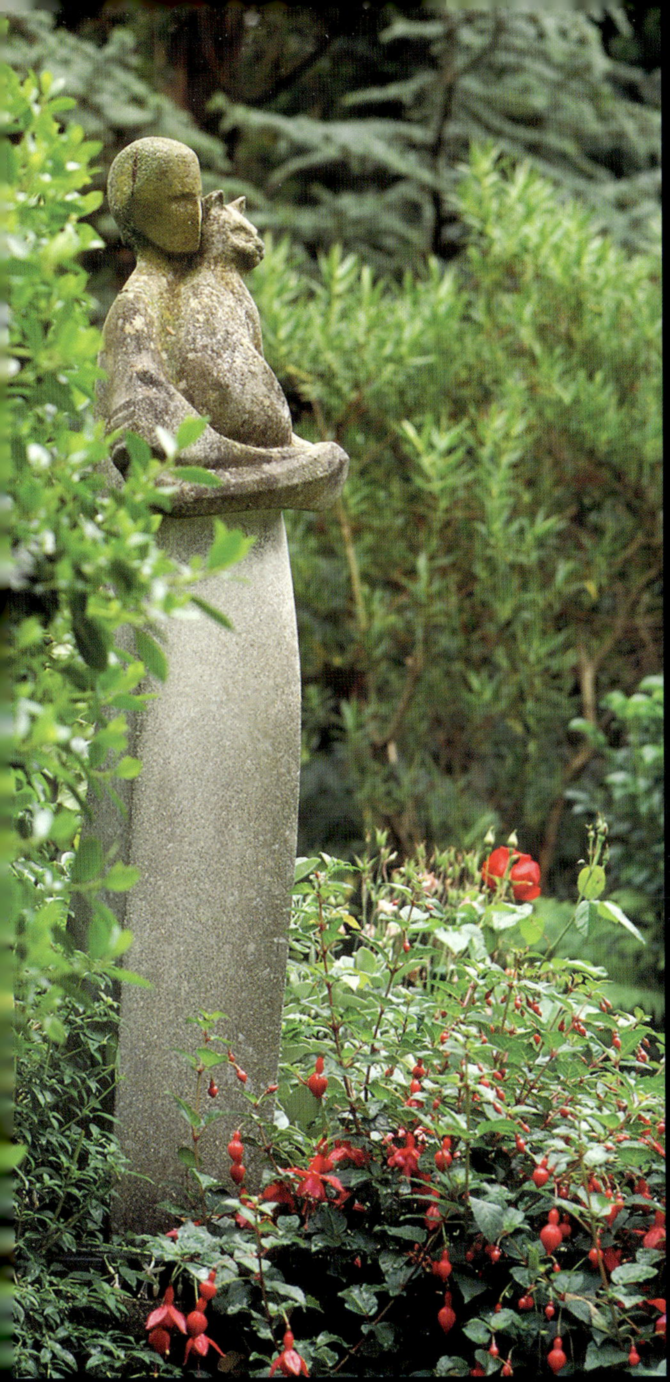

introduction

Carole Vincent is an artist whose chosen material is concrete. Few artists have so successfully exploited concrete's ability to be cast into free-form shapes, and none has infused it with such a dazzling spectrum of brilliant colours. Carole Vincent's sculptures range from small, personal pieces to large public commissions, environmental and garden designs, in which plants and sculptures are integrated to form a harmonious whole.

Concrete Works traces the development of Carole Vincent's work, showing it in the context of her home on the rugged coast of north Cornwall.

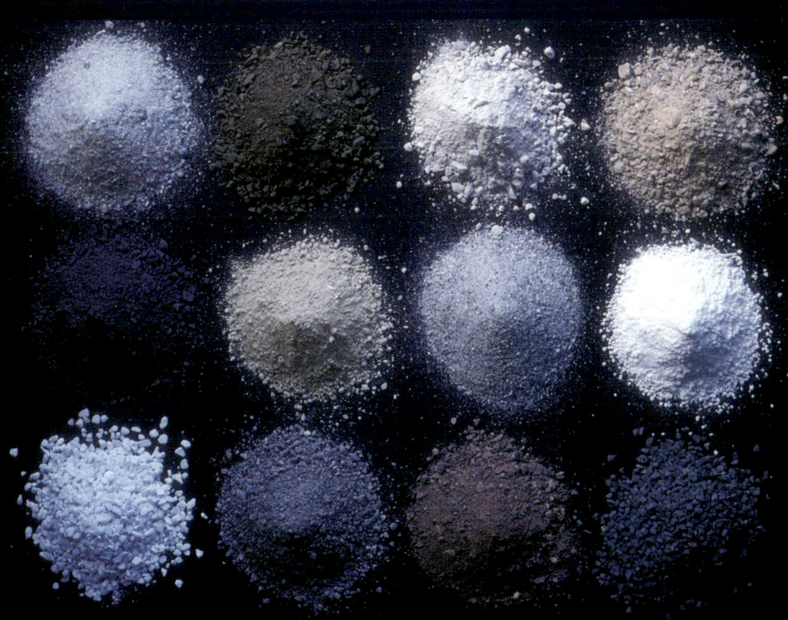

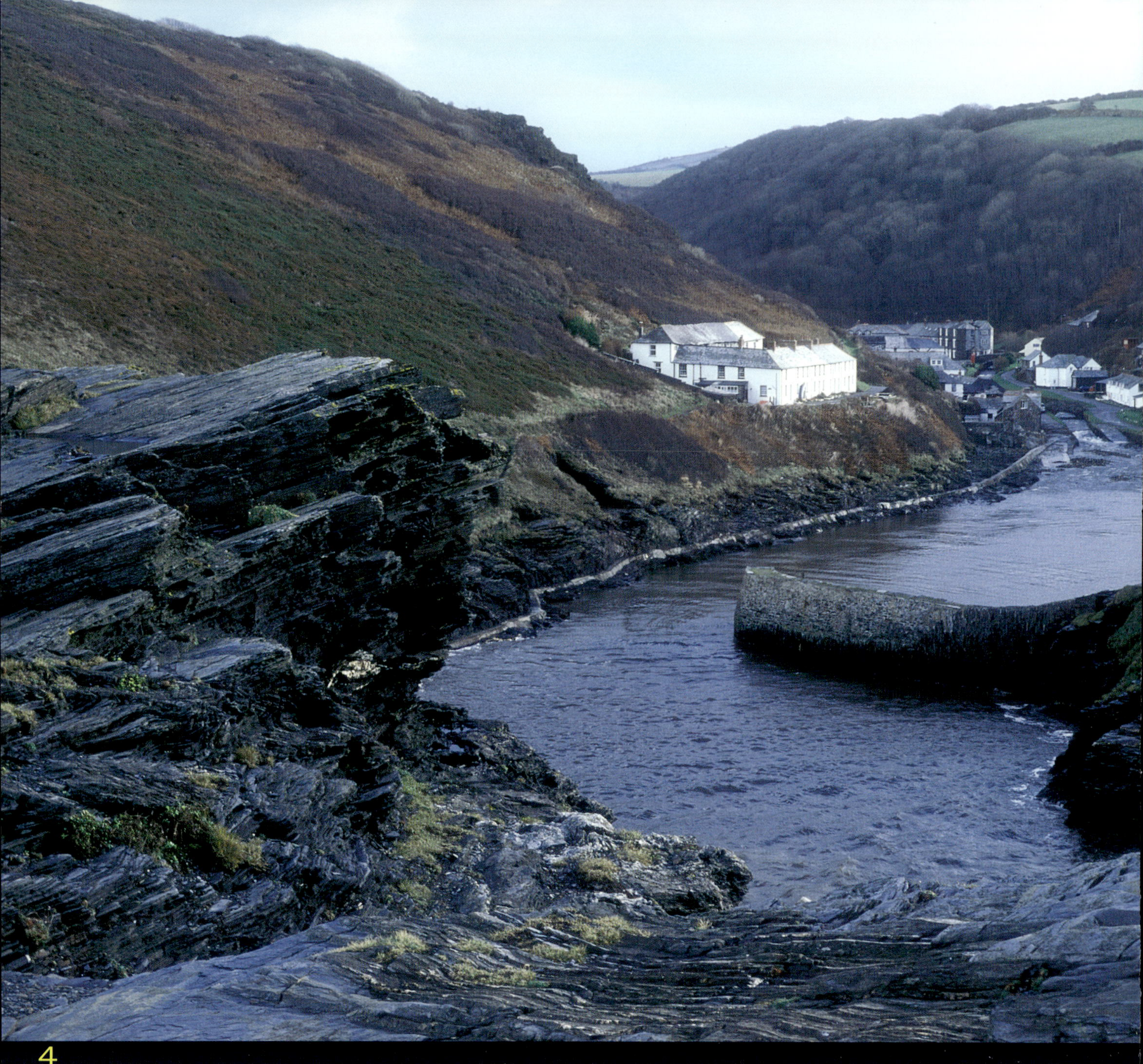

place of work

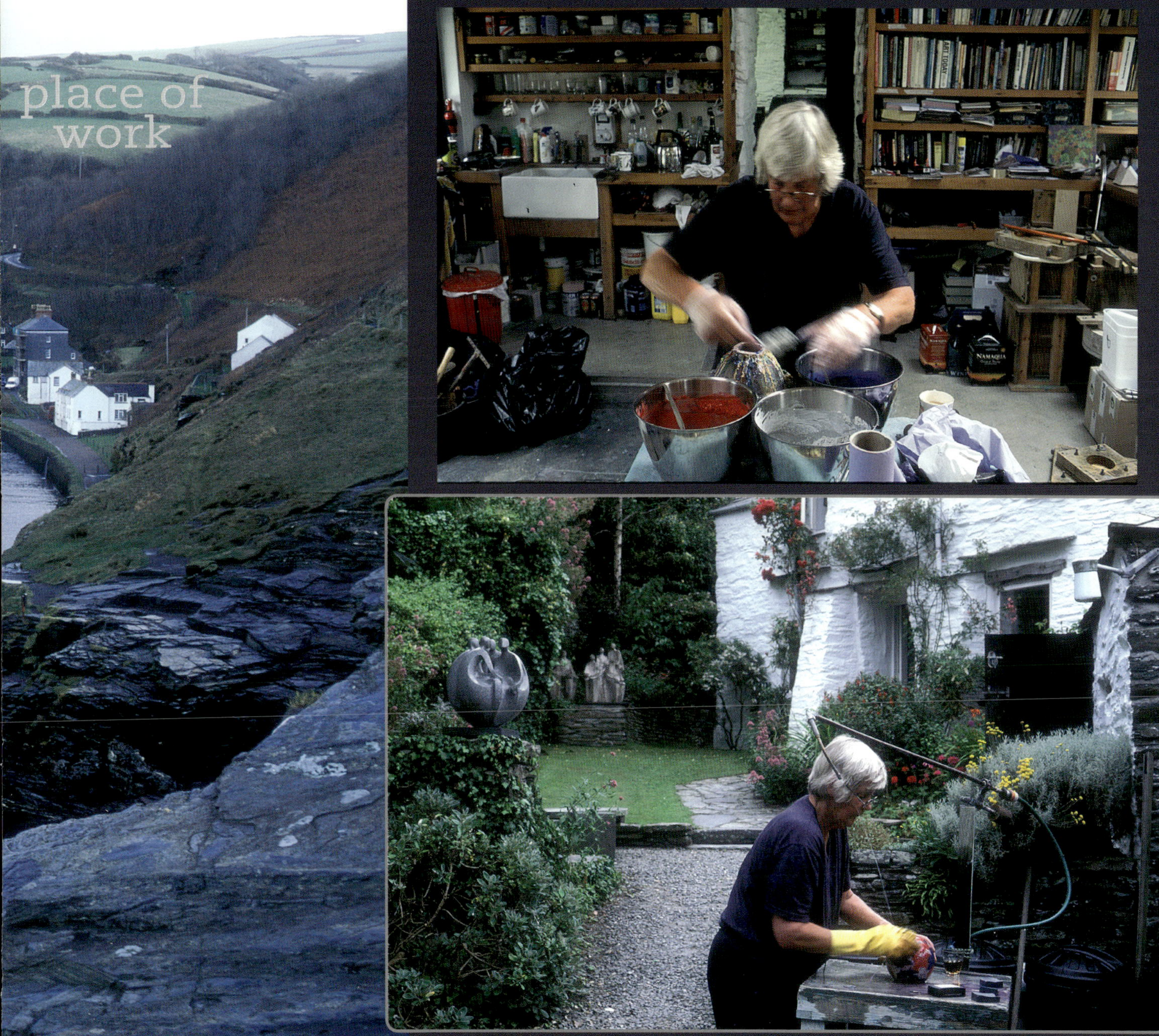

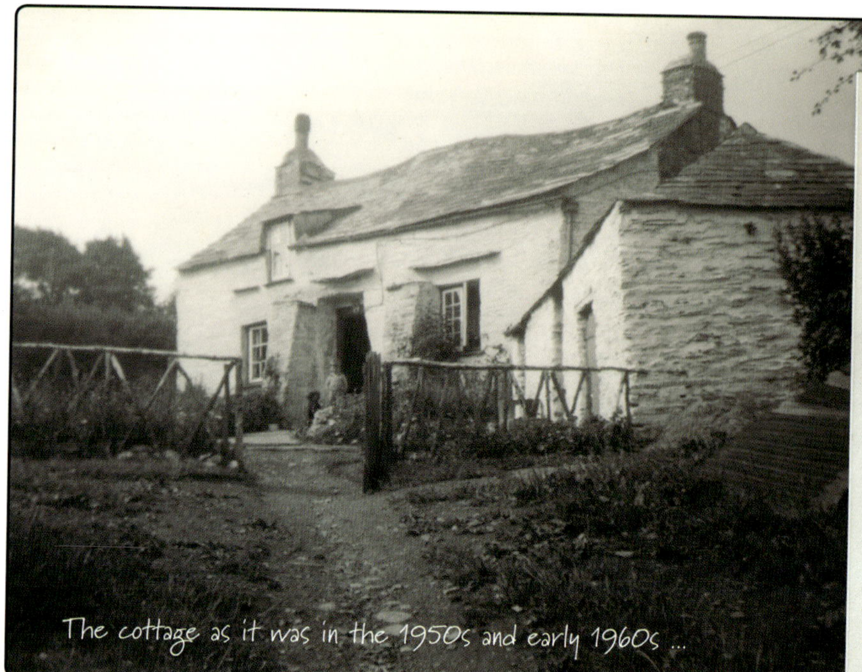

The cottage as it was in the 1950s and early 1960s ...

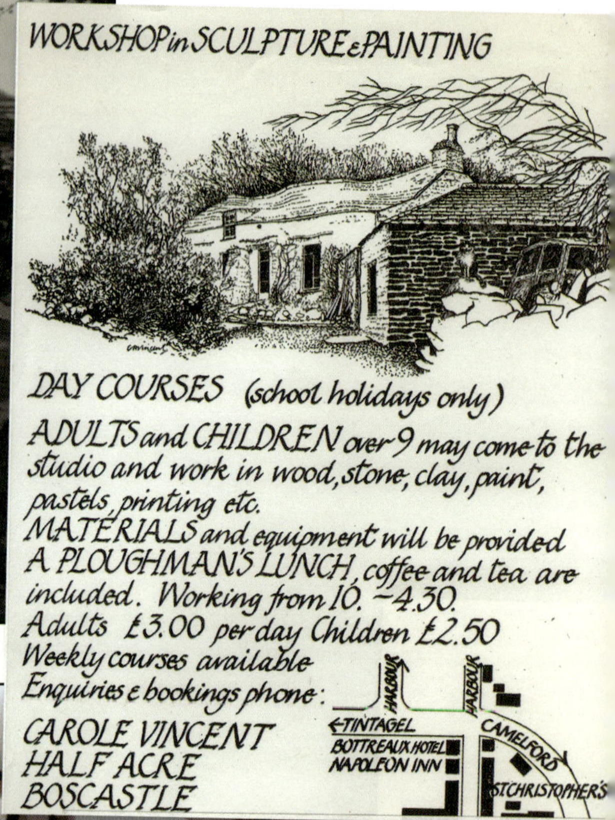

WORKSHOP in SCULPTURE & PAINTING

DAY COURSES (school holidays only)

ADULTS and CHILDREN over 9 may come to the studio and work in wood, stone, clay, paint, pastels, printing etc.

MATERIALS and equipment will be provided

A PLOUGHMAN'S LUNCH, coffee and tea are included. Working from 10. – 4.30.

Adults £3.00 per day Children £2.50

Weekly courses available

Enquiries & bookings phone:

CAROLE VINCENT
HALF ACRE
BOSCASTLE

HARBOUR
HARBOUR
←TINTAGEL
CAMELFORD
BOTTREAUX HOTEL
NAPOLEON INN
ST CHRISTOPHER'S

Carole Vincent was born in Crediton, Devon, the daughter of a builder. From the age of nine she made blocks in the family concrete works – little thinking where it would lead. After training at the Bath Academy of Art, she settled in Boscastle, North Cornwall, where she has lived and worked ever since, as sculptor, painter and teacher.

Half Acre – her home and studio – is a cottage built of local slate, overlooking the village. She bought it in 1967, and since then has extended and enlarged it to provide studio space for her own work, and for the summer holiday classes that she has run since 1971.

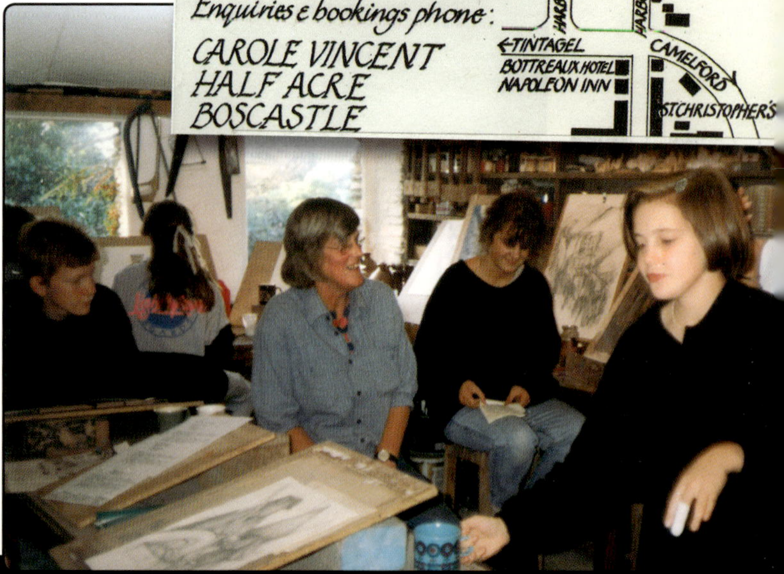

A holiday class in the mid-1970s.

Half Acre – a cottage by the sea

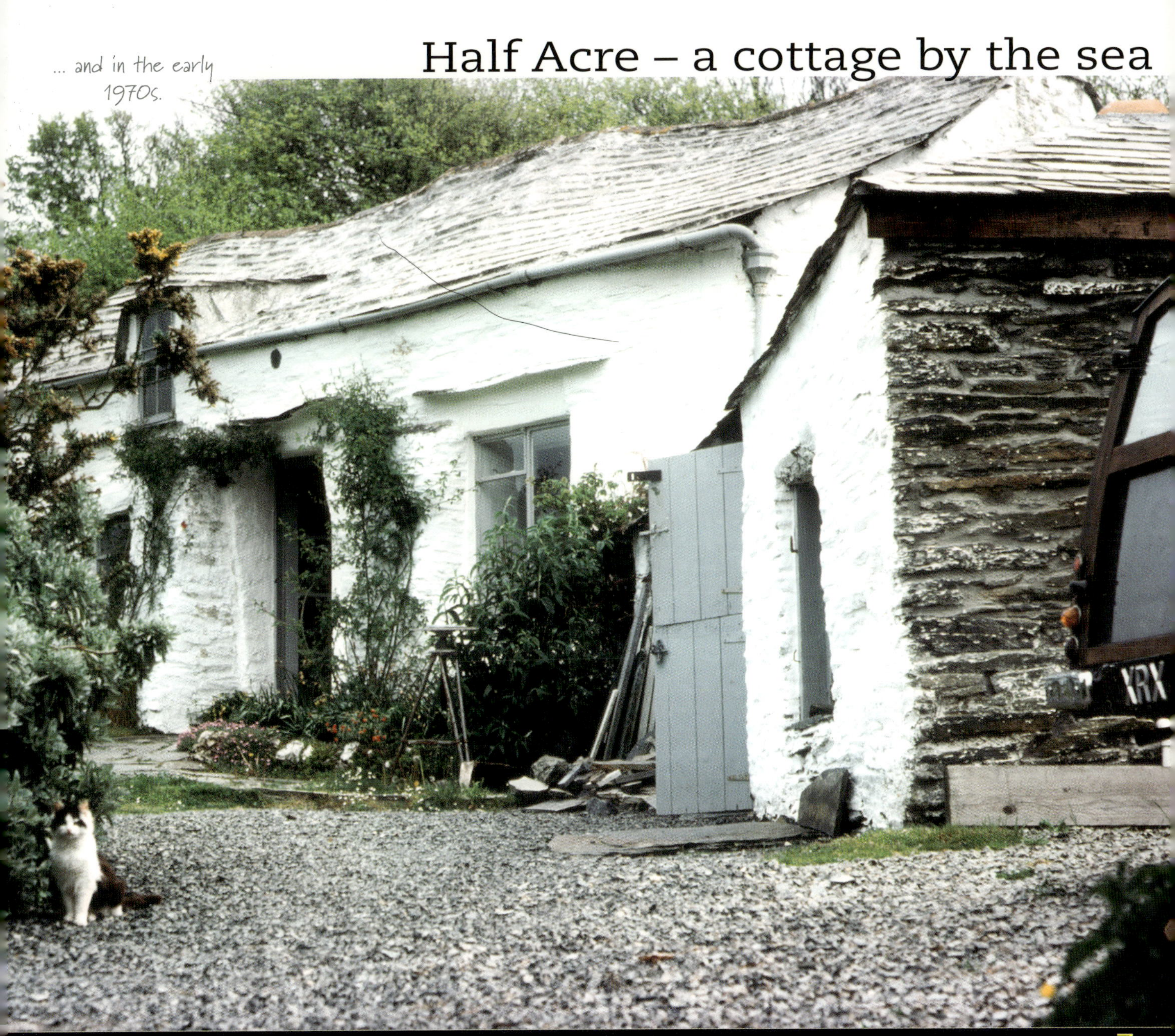

... and in the early 1970s.

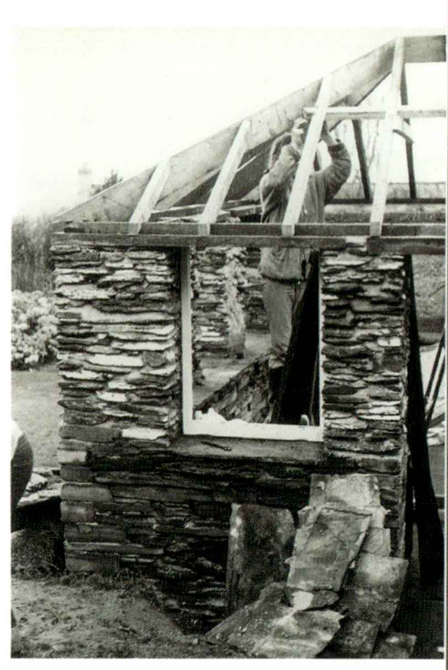

I did much of the early construction work myself, occasionally asking Father for advice and having the help of friends for two-man jobs. ...

... From 1975 to 1978 the garden grew, the classes grew ... and my work developed.

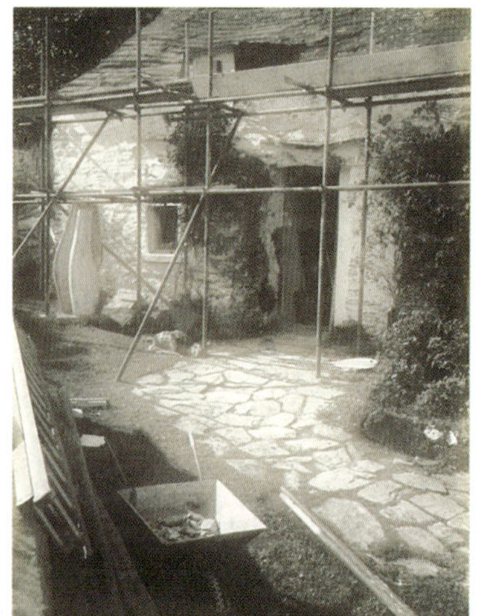

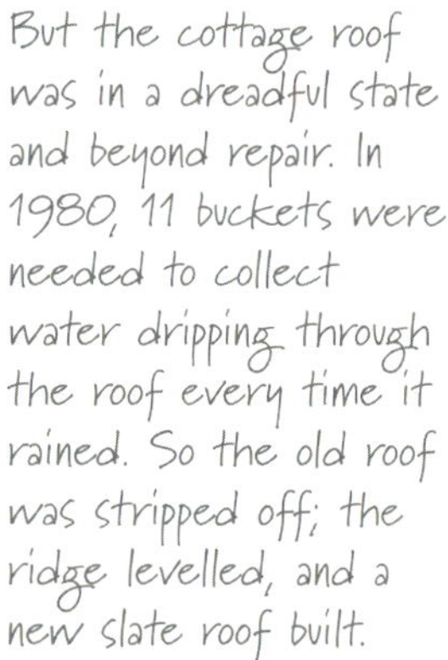

But the cottage roof was in a dreadful state and beyond repair. In 1980, 11 buckets were needed to collect water dripping through the roof every time it rained. So the old roof was stripped off; the ridge levelled, and a new slate roof built.

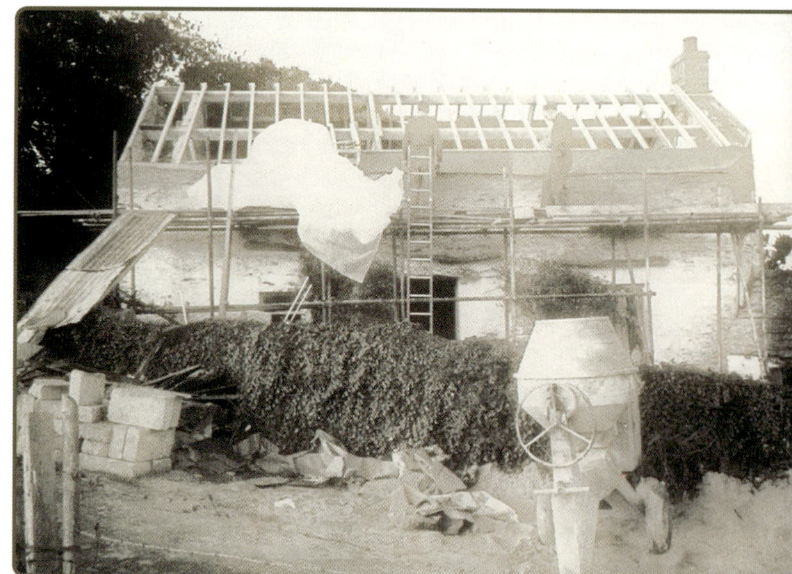

building a dream

For many years I dreamed of a large, light studio, purpose-built for sculpture. In 1989, with the purchase of an adjoining field, it became possible to build it. Every day it became more beautiful. September 23rd marked the completion of the new studio. I celebrated my 50th birthday and 28 years at Half Acre.

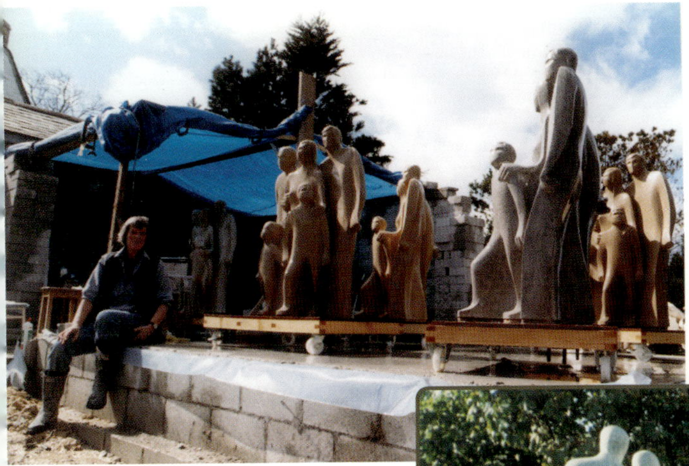

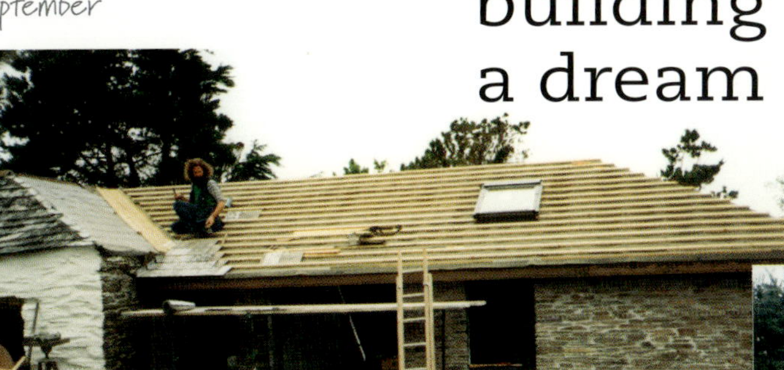

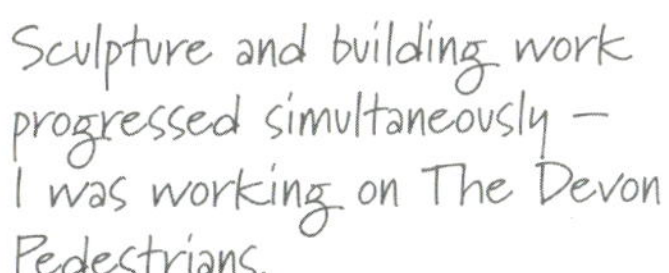

Sculpture and building work progressed simultaneously – I was working on The Devon Pedestrians.

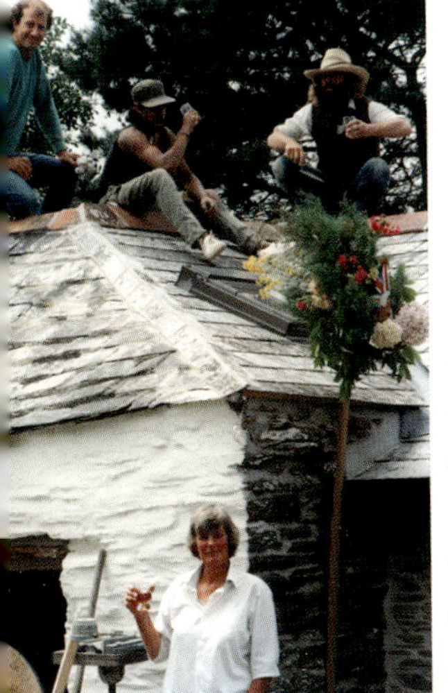

topping out ceremony

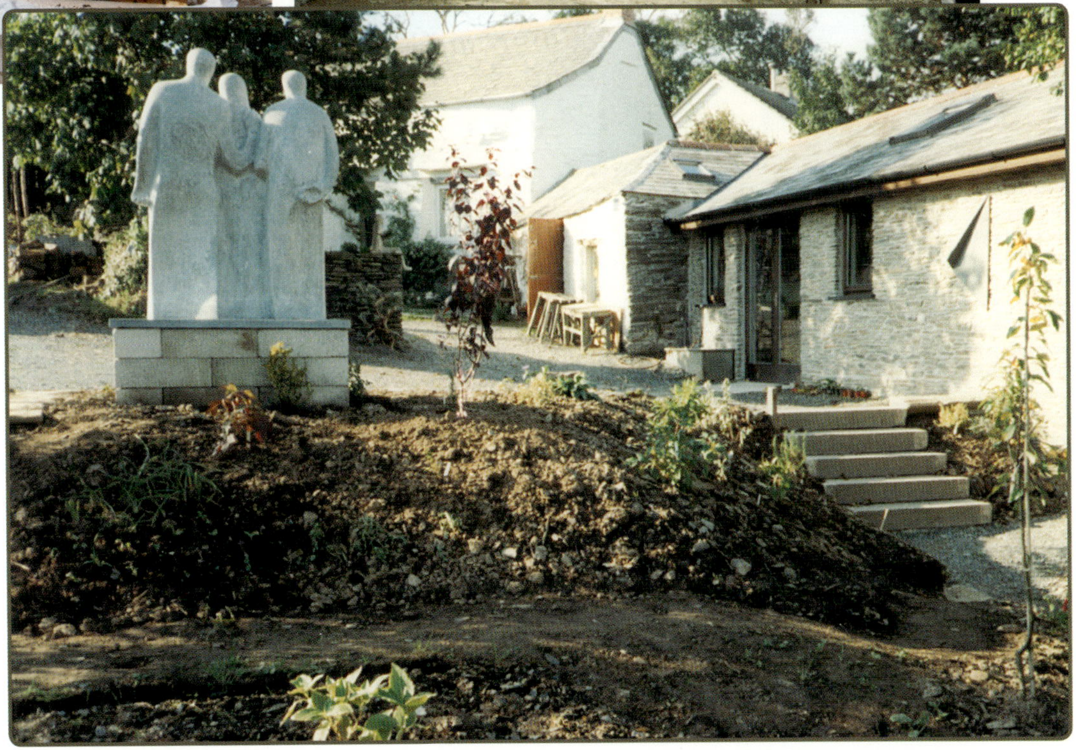

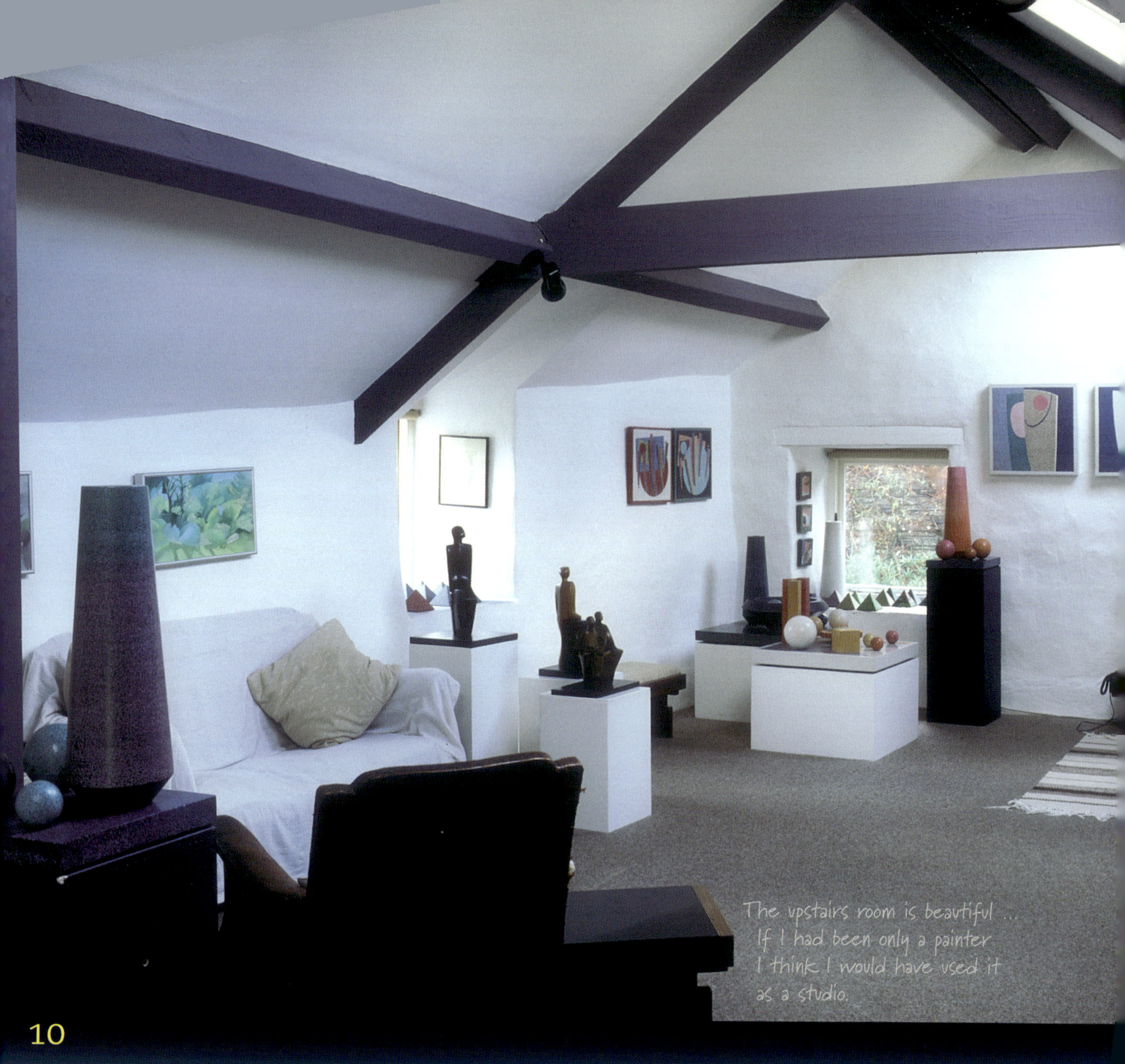

The upstairs room is beautiful ... If I had been only a painter I think I would have used it as a studio.

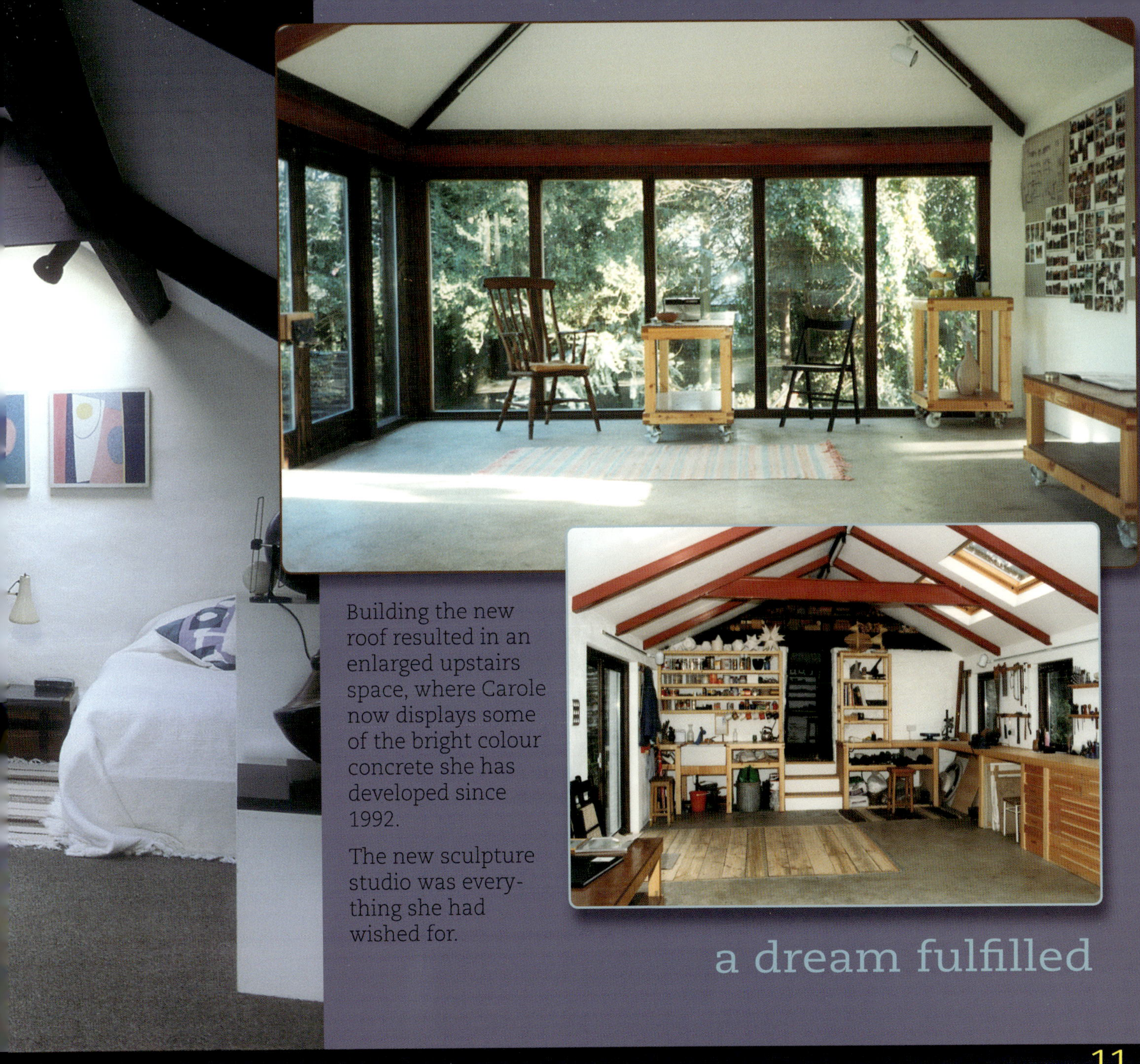

Building the new roof resulted in an enlarged upstairs space, where Carole now displays some of the bright colour concrete she has developed since 1992.

The new sculpture studio was everything she had wished for.

a dream fulfilled

garden and sculpture

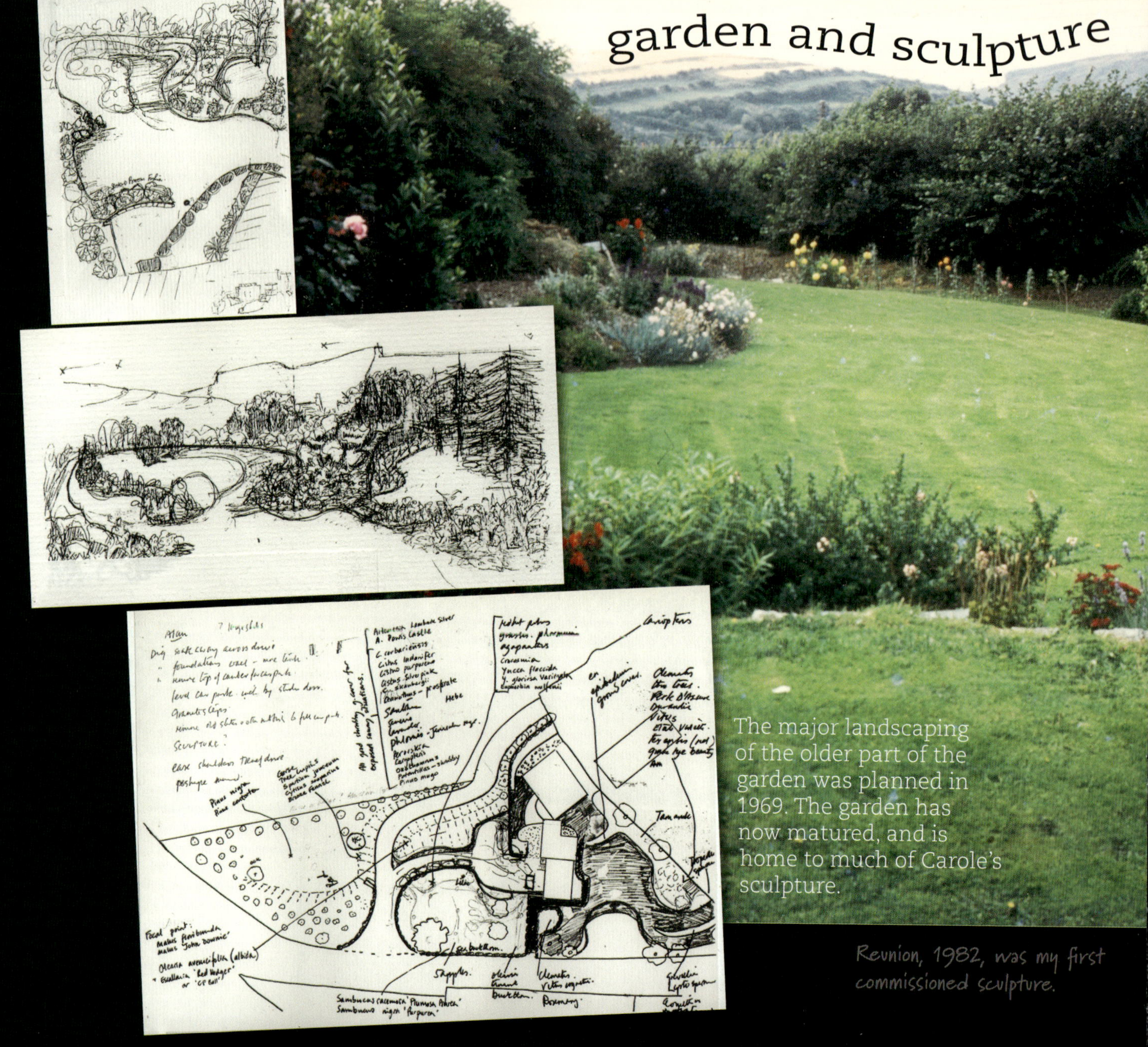

The major landscaping of the older part of the garden was planned in 1969. The garden has now matured, and is home to much of Carole's sculpture.

Reunion, 1982, was my first commissioned sculpture.

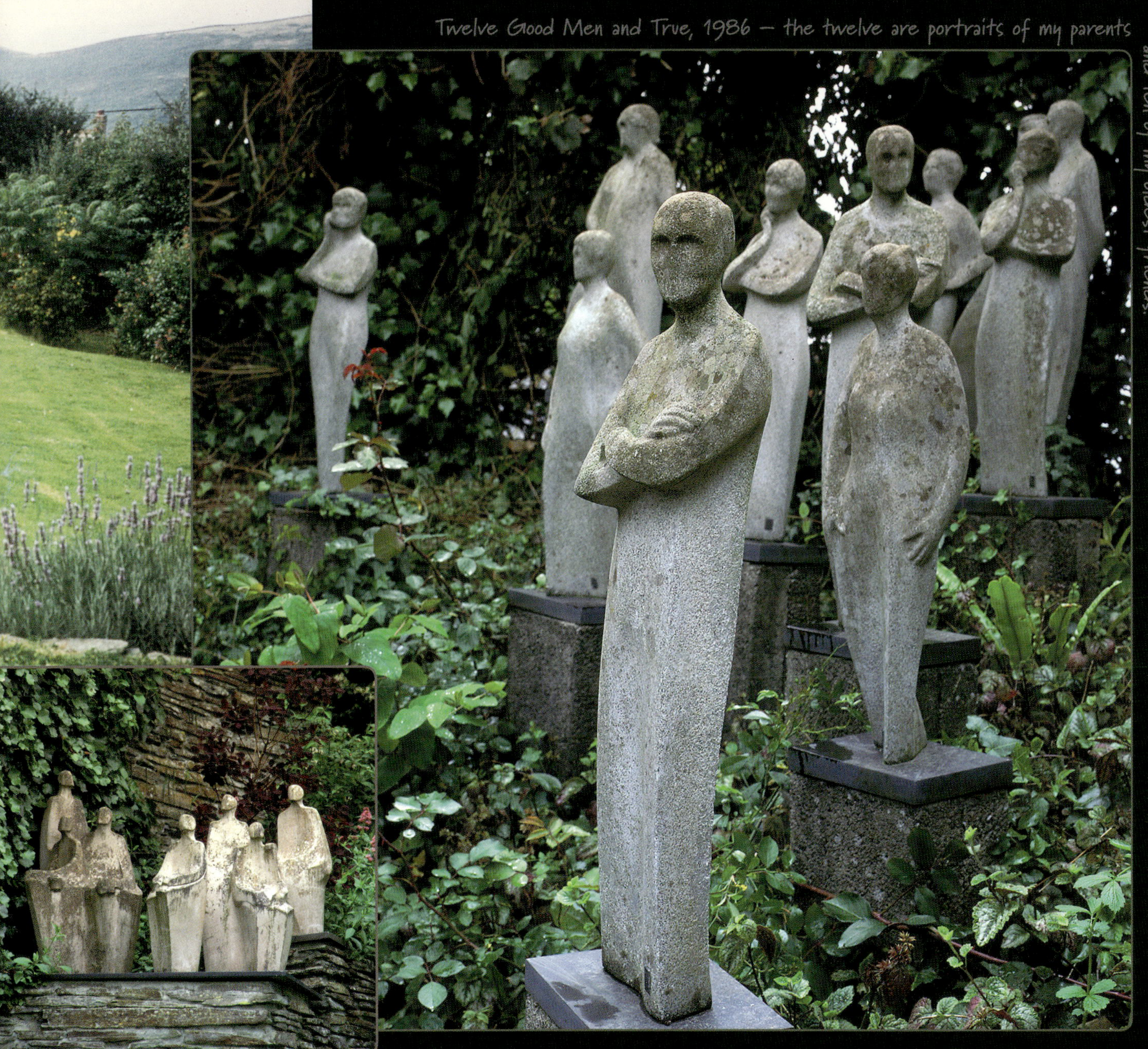

Twelve Good Men and True, 1986 – the twelve are portraits of my parents and ten of my oldest friends.

The Devon Pedestrians, 1989, marked a significant change in my working practice. My builder's yard became a laboratory where everything is carefully weighed and measured.

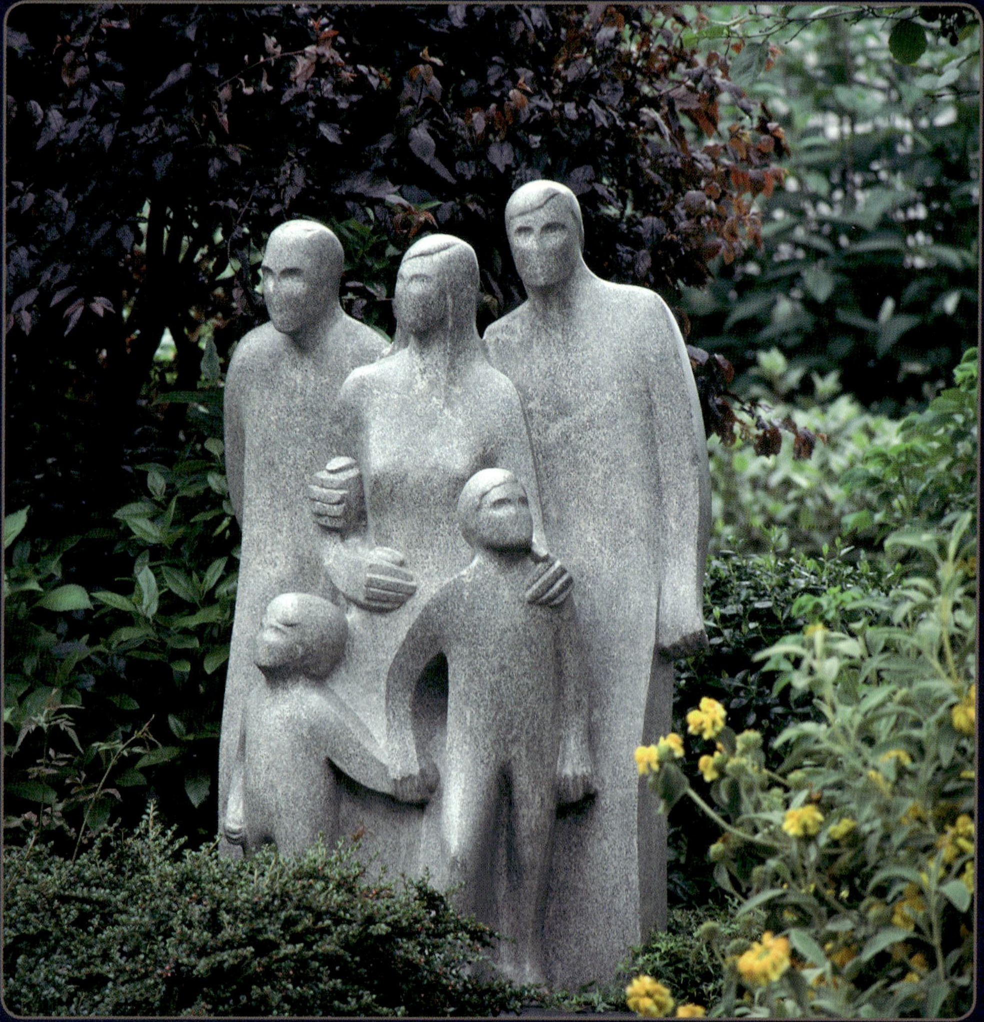

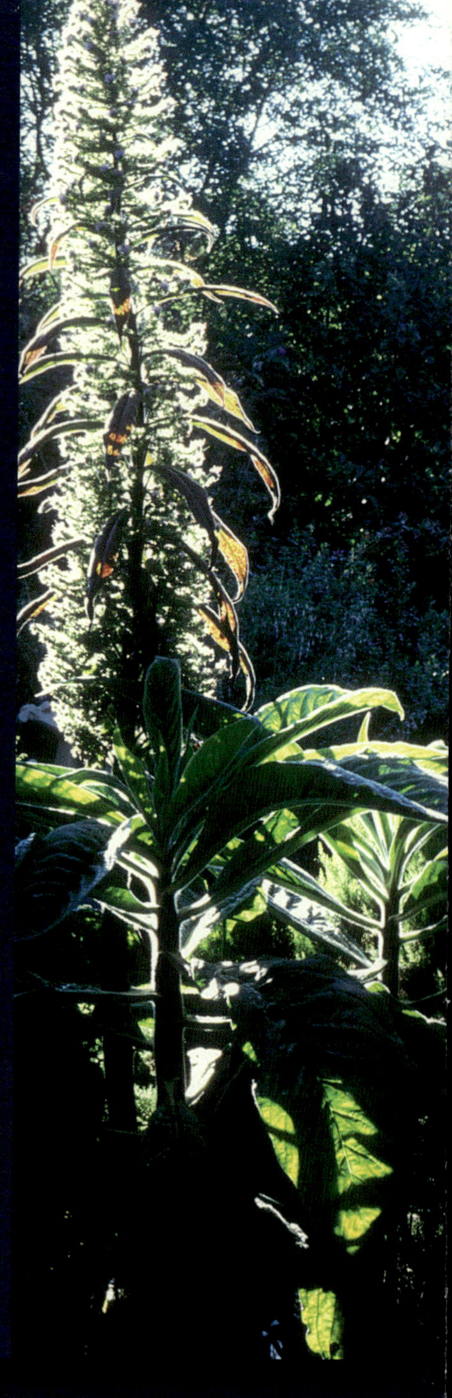

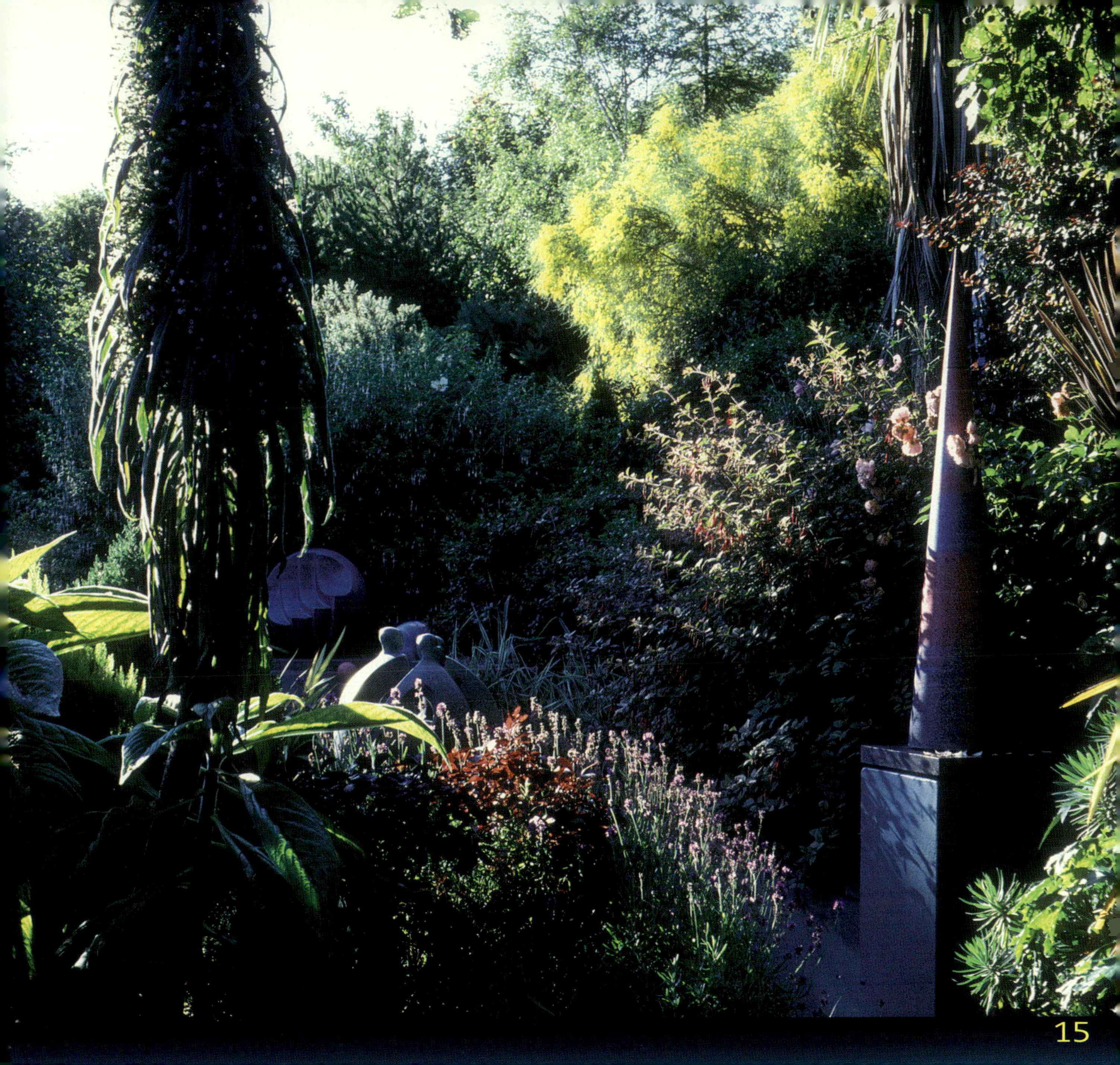

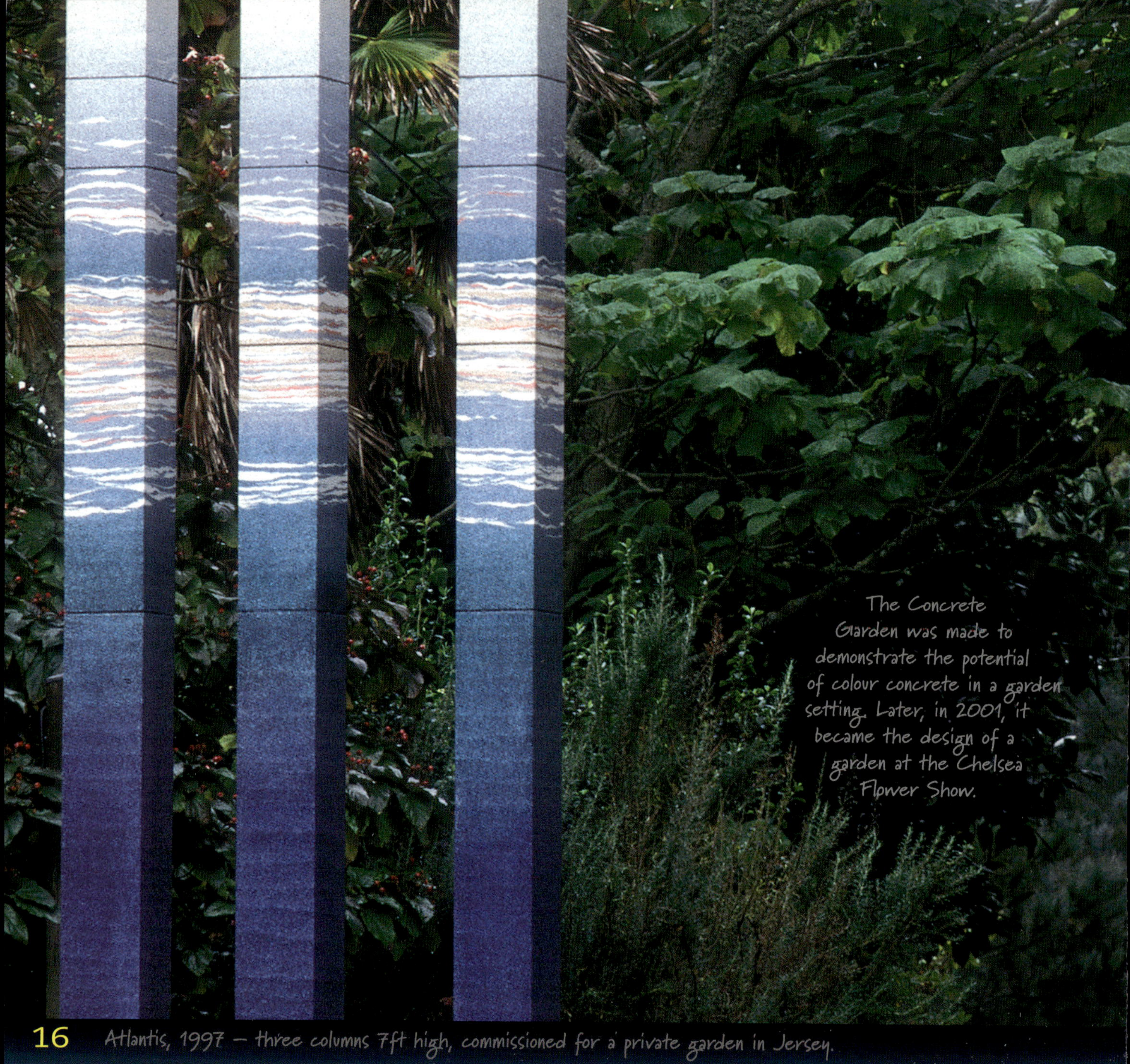

The Concrete Garden was made to demonstrate the potential of colour concrete in a garden setting. Later, in 2001, it became the design of a garden at the Chelsea Flower Show.

Atlantis, 1997 – three columns 7ft high, commissioned for a private garden in Jersey.

the Concrete Garden

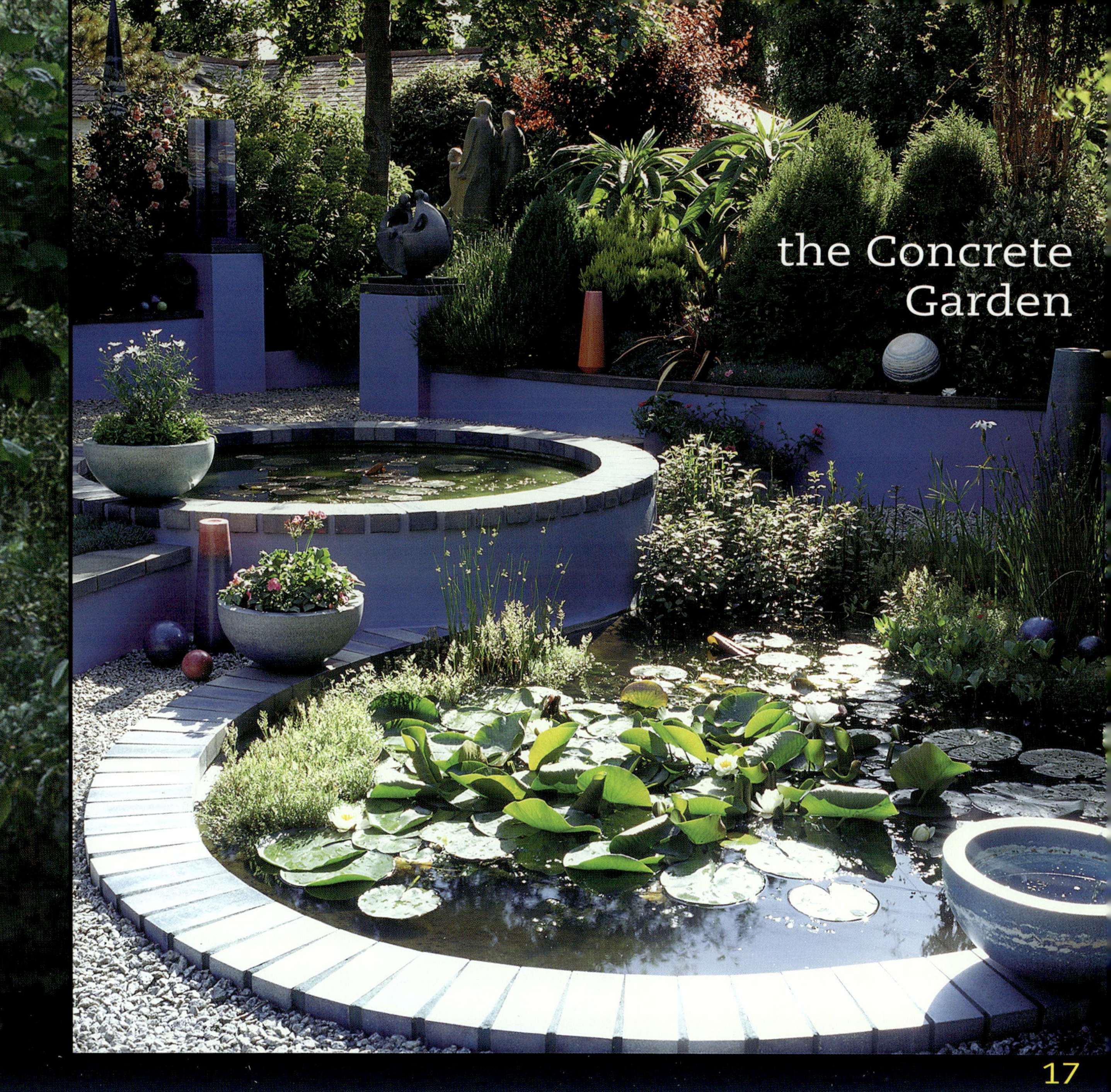

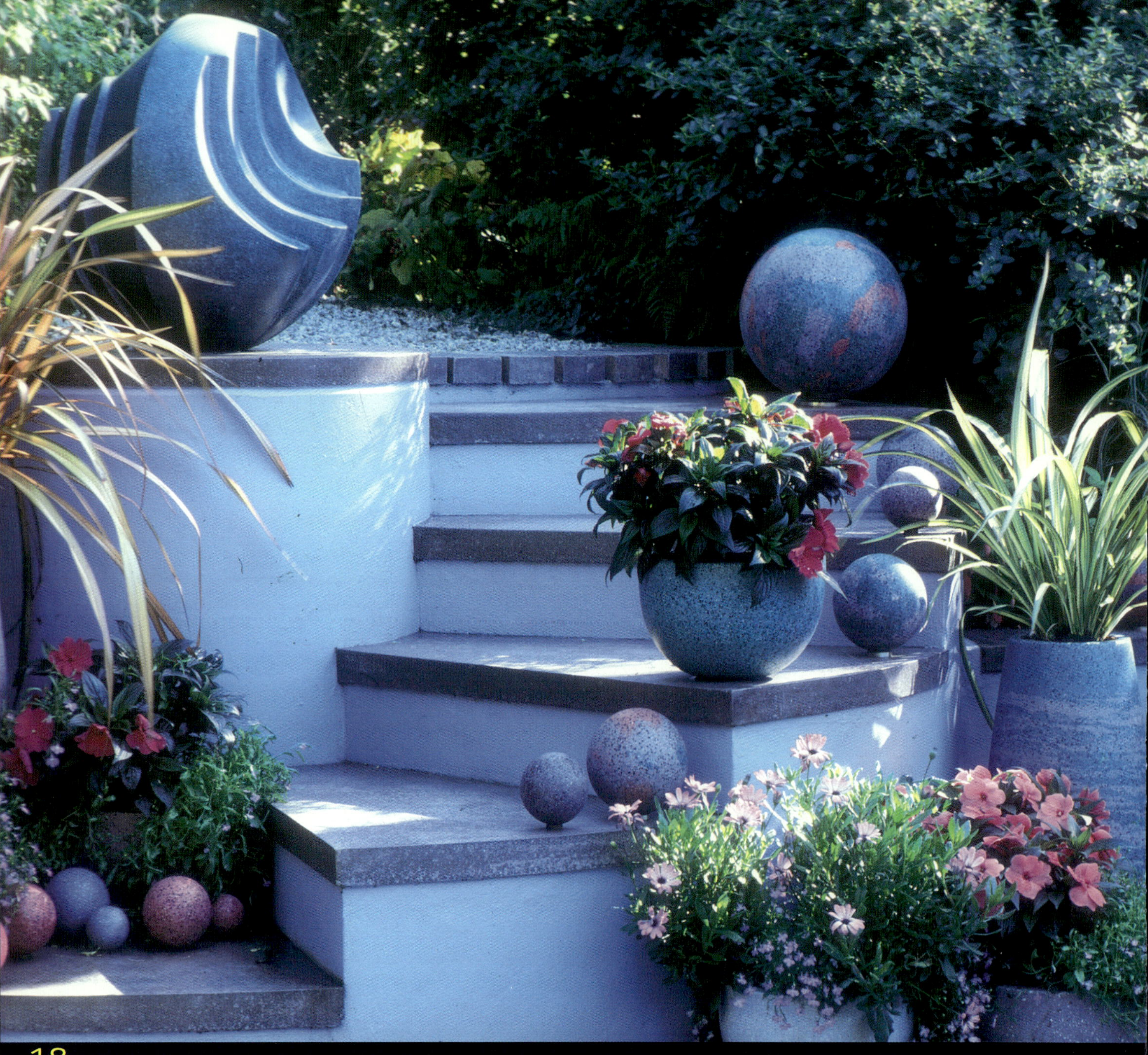

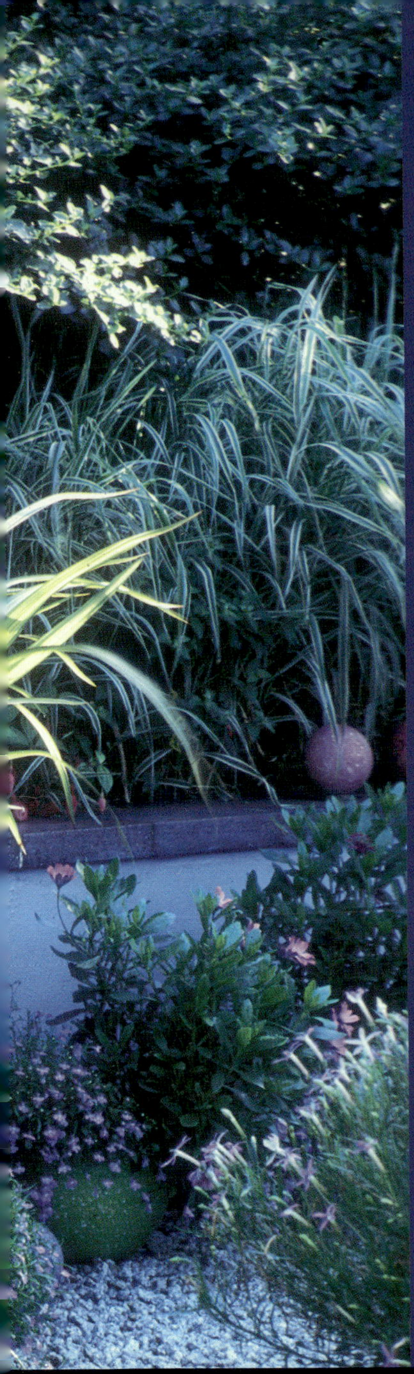

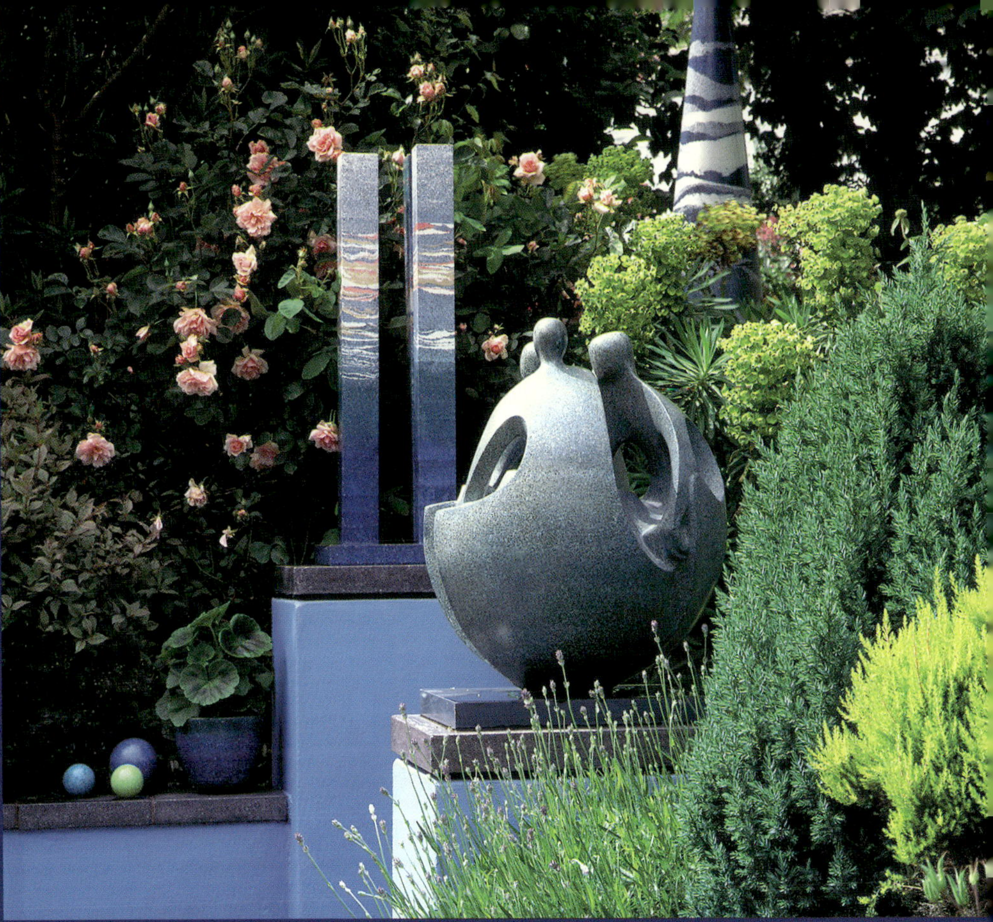

Concrete and plants work in harmony.

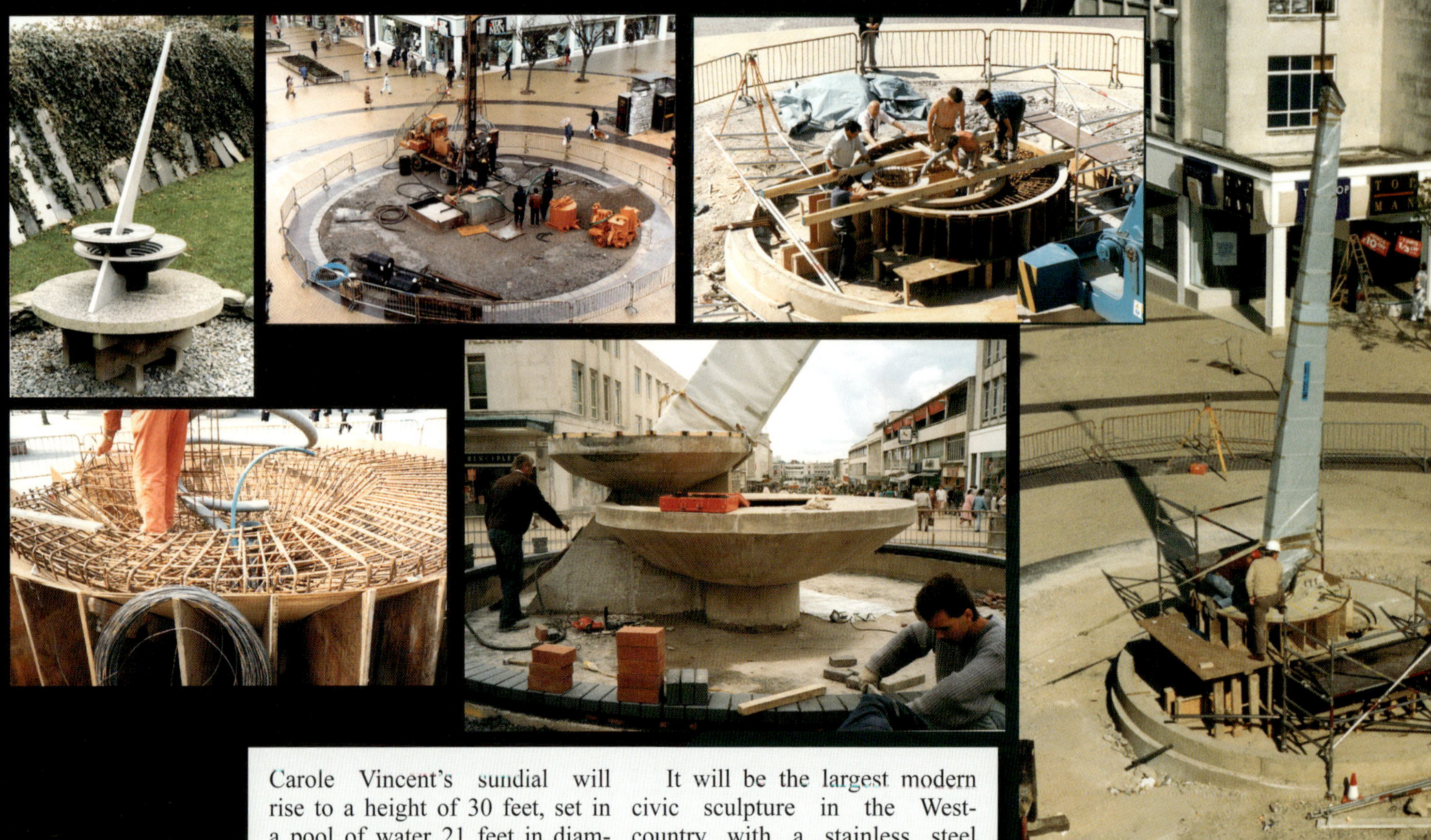

Carole Vincent's sundial will rise to a height of 30 feet, set in a pool of water 21 feet in diameter at the junction of Armada Way and New George Street.

Plymouth City Council have selected the design from a choice of five proposals. Miss Vincent's idea had over 50 per cent of the public vote when the models were displayed in the Civic Centre. Now the decision has been made the City Engineers Department has to complete the specifications of the full size sundial which will weigh about 12½ cwt and cost over £50,000 to build....

It will be the largest modern civic sculpture in the West-country with a stainless steel gnomon which casts the shadow on the hour lines 33 feet long.

Water will cascade over the dial and there will be stools to sit on which will mark the hours.

The gnomon will look like a steel sail and the whole sculpture will have the feeling of a sailing ship. It will be functional – people will be able to tell Plymouth local time – and be a meeting place for people.

(*Western Morning News*, 09/87)

The controversial Armada sundial proved to be a major talking point for the Queen on her Plymouth visit. The 30 foot high landmark which has been described as a monstrosity and a waste of money was unveiled by the Queen.

(*The Post & Weekly News*)

the Armada Dial

Carole's first large public commission came in 1998. The Armada Dial was commissioned by Plymouth City Council for the junction of Armada Way and New George Street, as the centrepiece for the revitalization of the city.

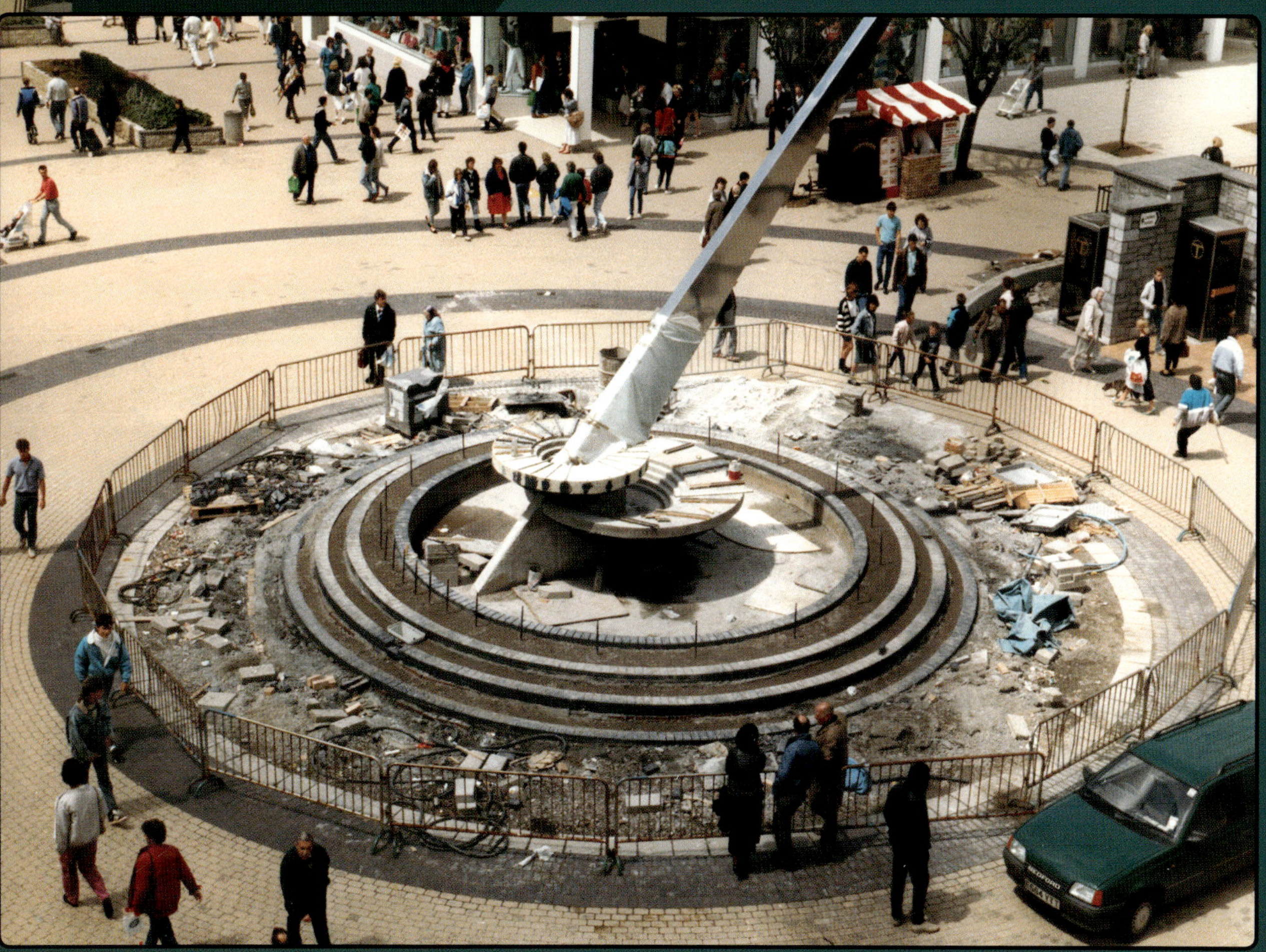

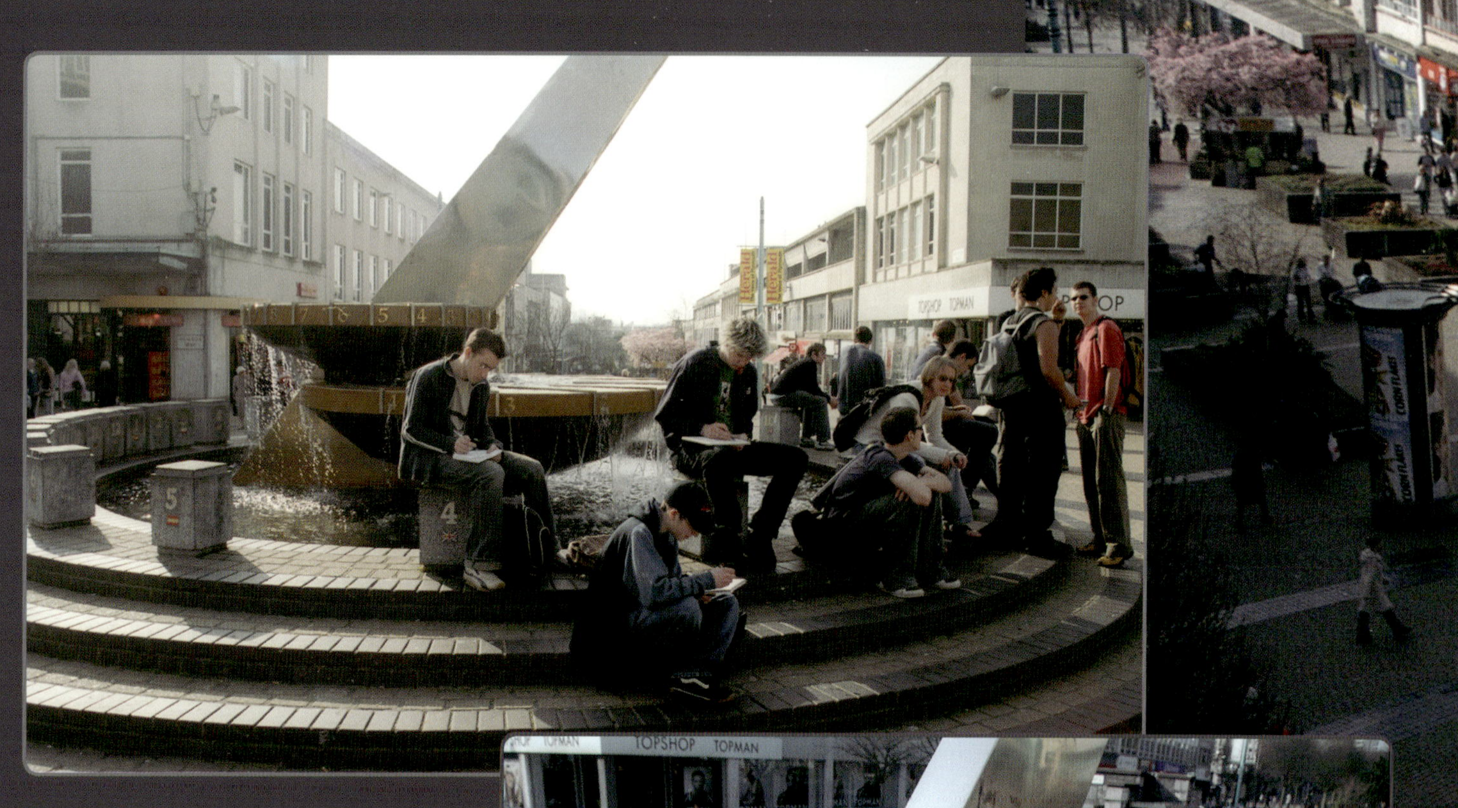

The Armada Dial was dedicated to the Armada 400 celebrations by HM Queen Elizabeth II in July 1988.

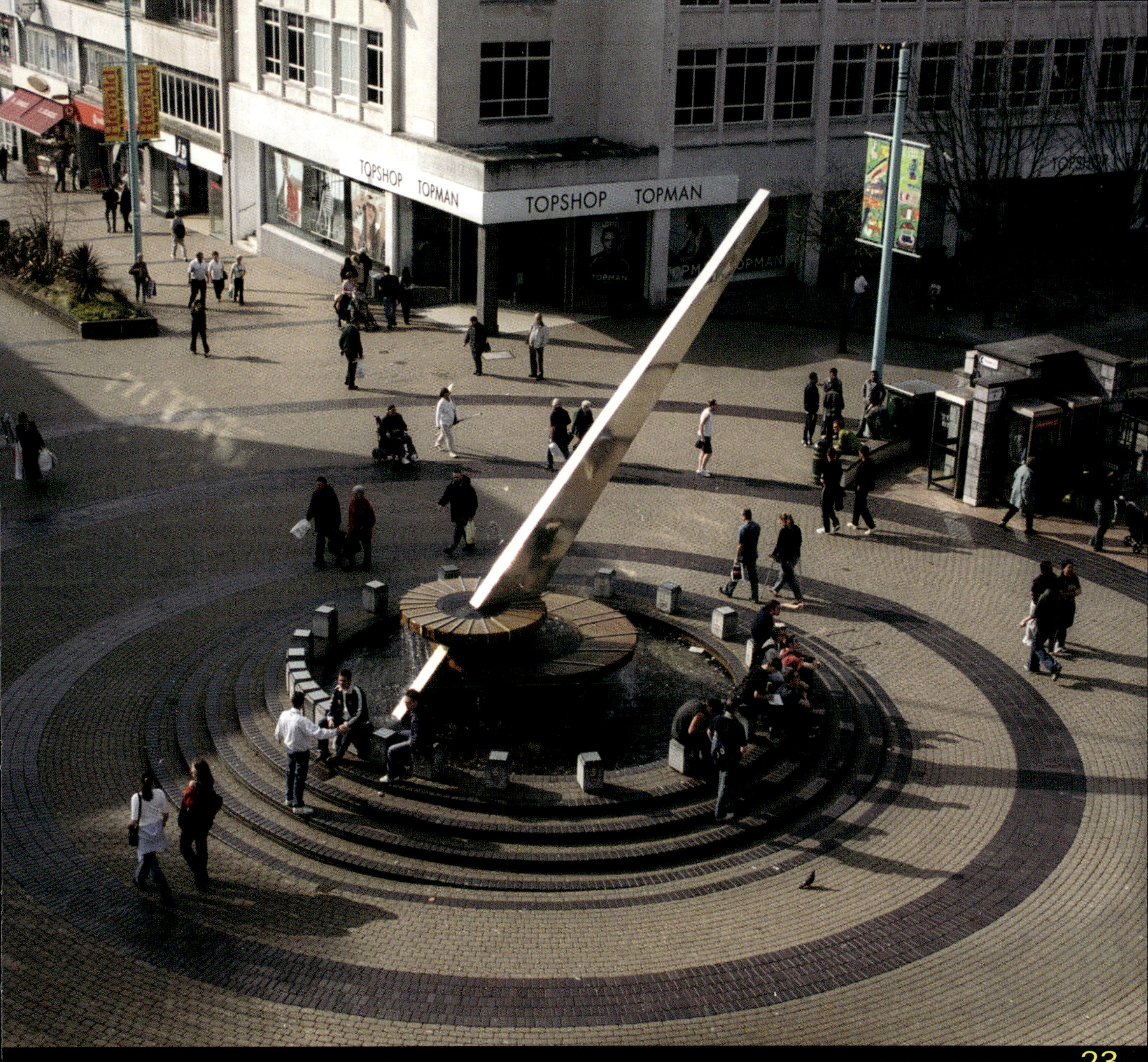
TOPSHOP TOPMAN
TOPSHOP
TOPMAN
Herald
Herald

The idea of a group of musicians took the form of a quartet because of the quartet's strong associations with Schubert and TS Eliot. Most figure sculptures have a front and a back, and the orthodox arrangement of a quartet would have produced this. The idea of setting three players around a central standing figure came during the modelling of the maquette. It seemed to provide a unity, a totally three-dimensional form which echoed the completeness of Schubert's music.

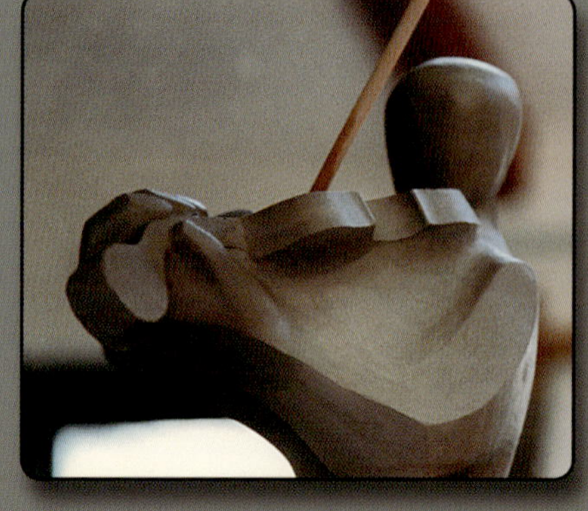

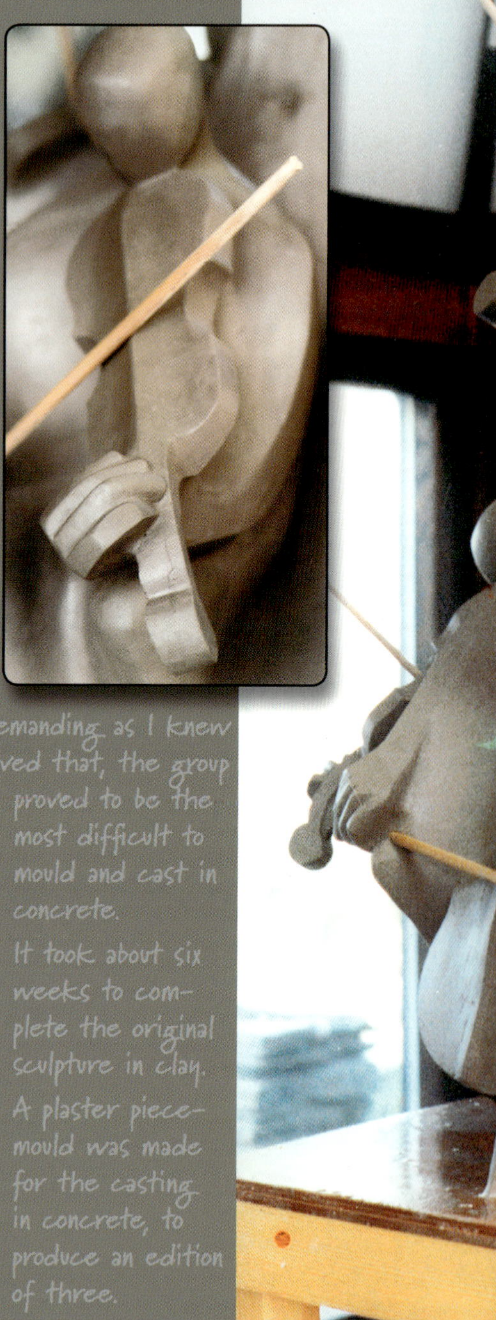

It was a luxury to be working on a private commission ... Working on a sculpture three feet high was more intimate – large enough to define detail, but not intimidating in its proportions for casting in concrete. Nevertheless it was ambitious and technically demanding as I knew little about playing stringed instruments, and having solved that, the group proved to be the most difficult to mould and cast in concrete.

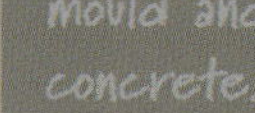

It took about six weeks to complete the original sculpture in clay.

A plaster piece-mould was made for the casting in concrete, to produce an edition of three.

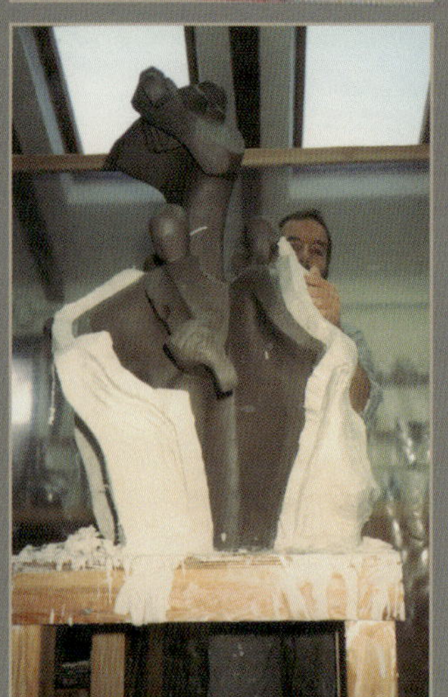

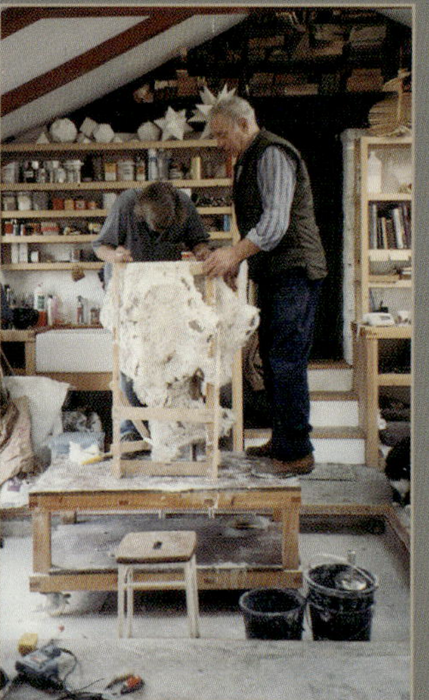

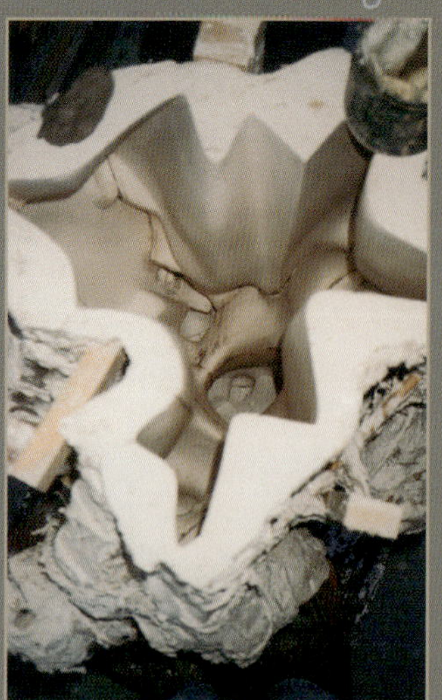

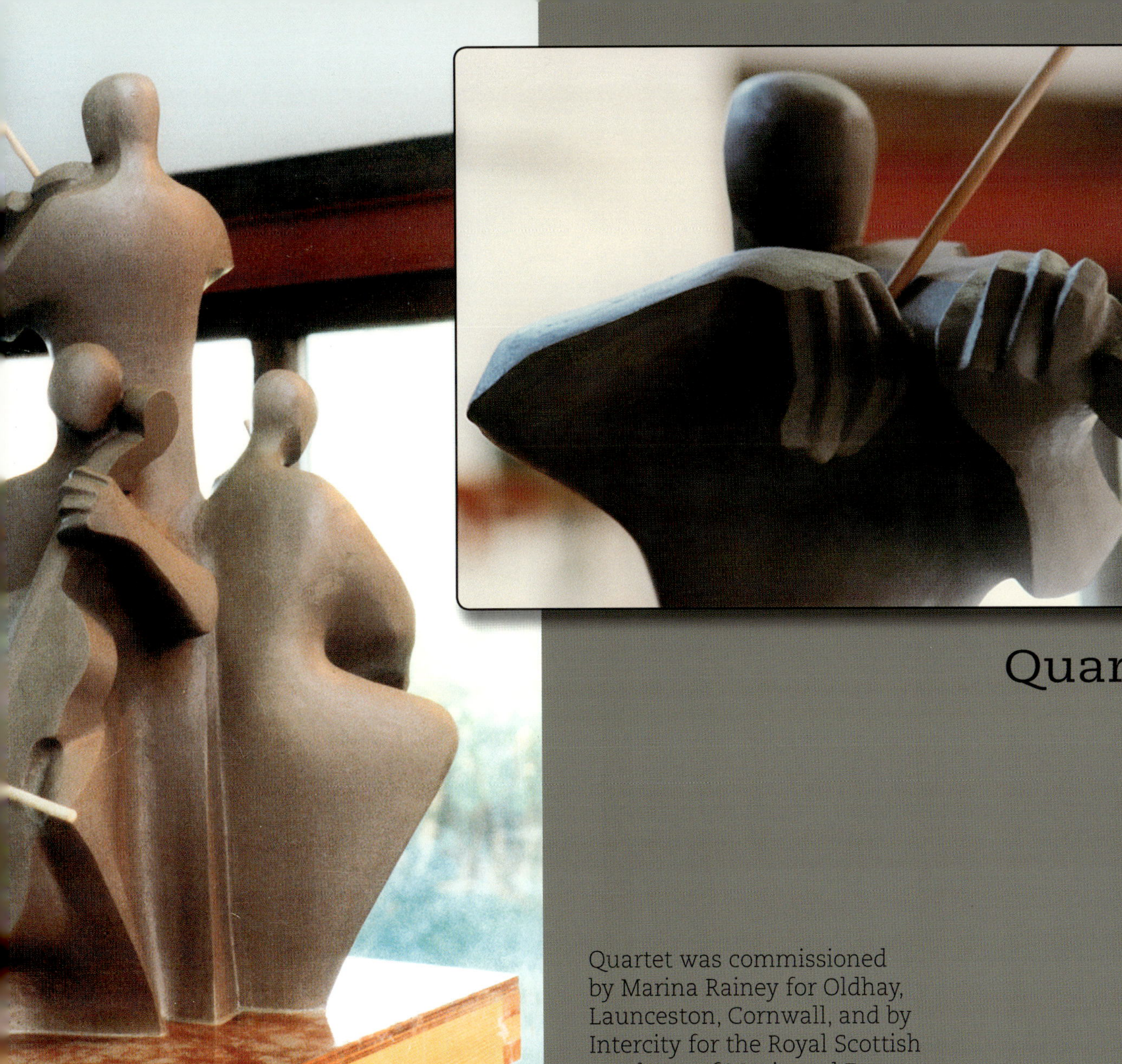

Quartet

Quartet was commissioned by Marina Rainey for Oldhay, Launceston, Cornwall, and by Intercity for the Royal Scottish Academy of Music and Drama in 1991.

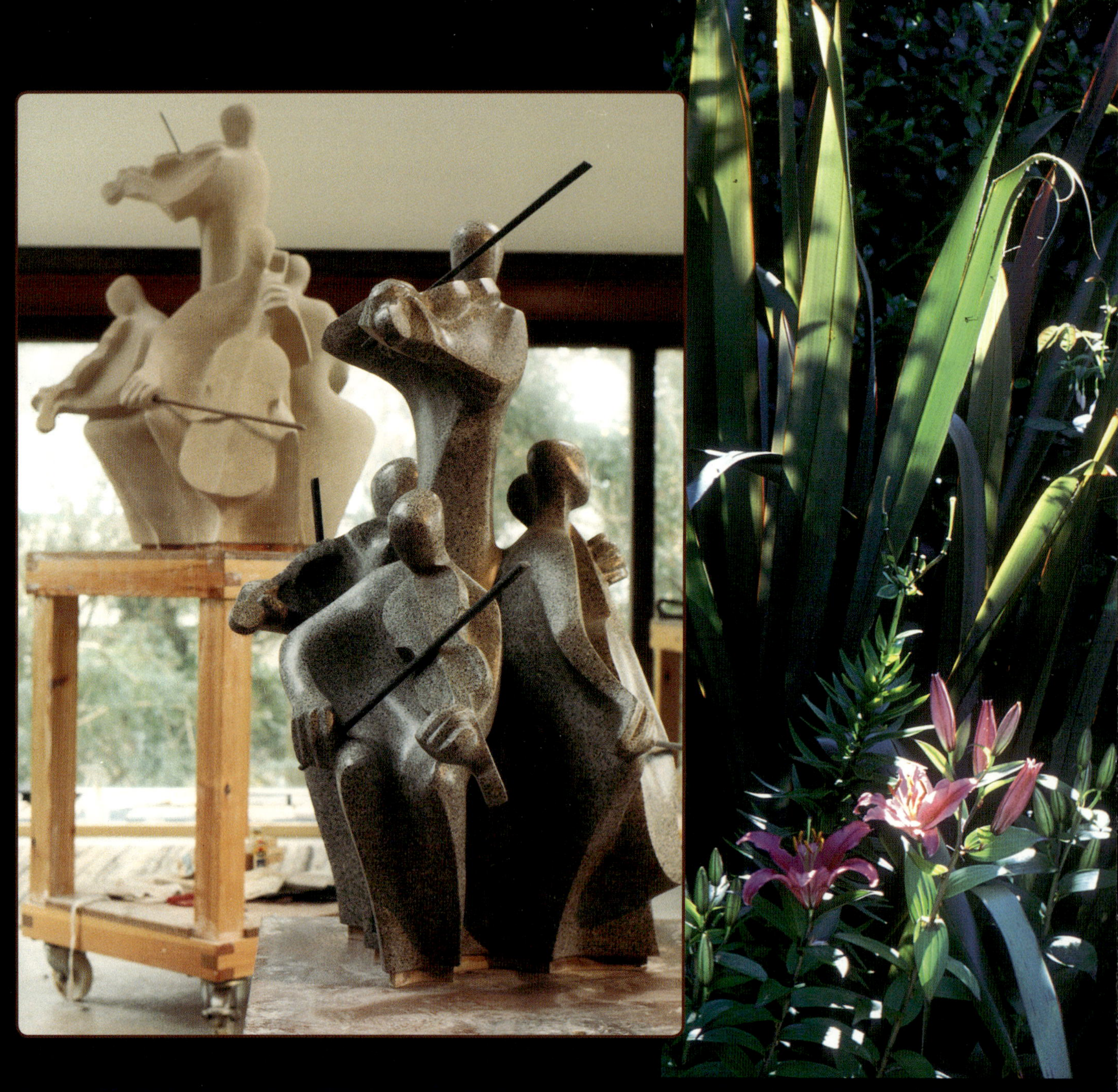

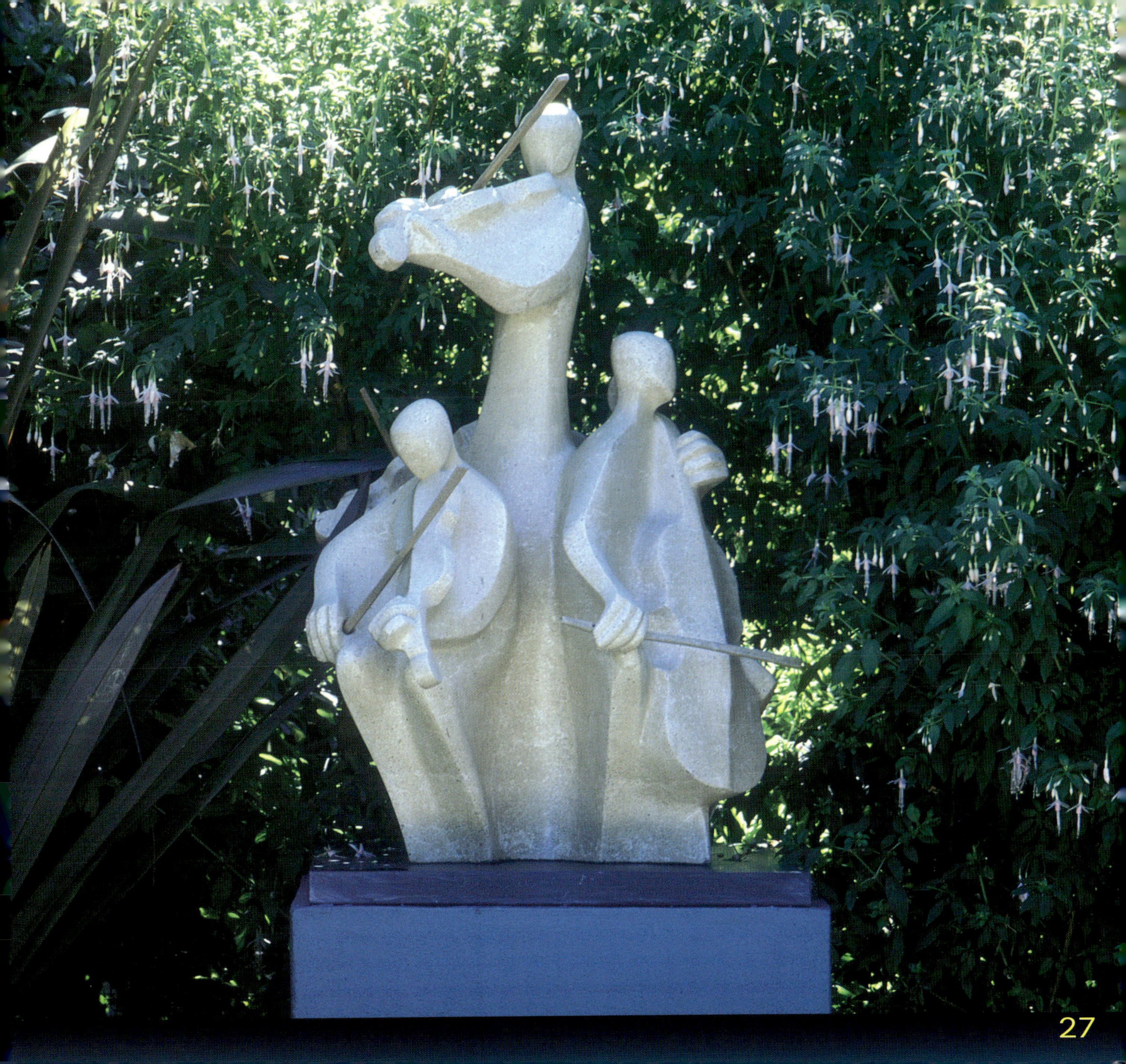

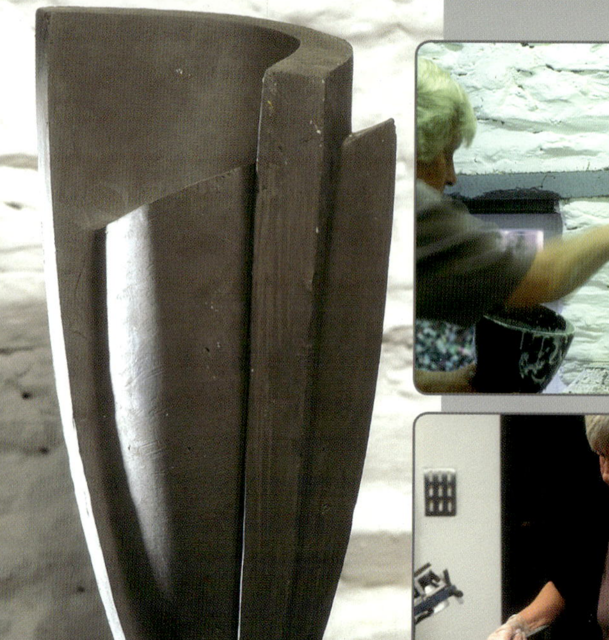
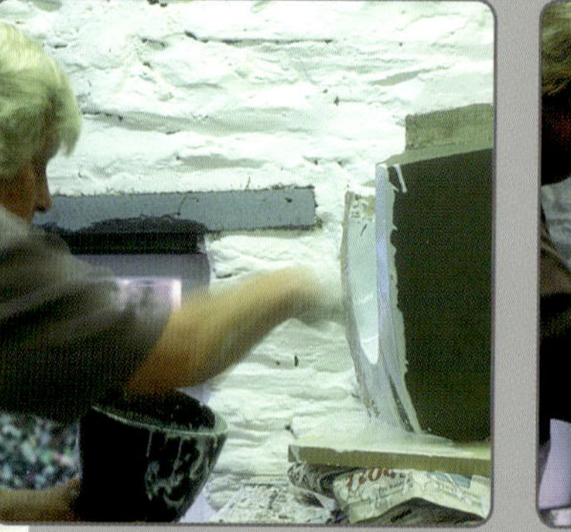
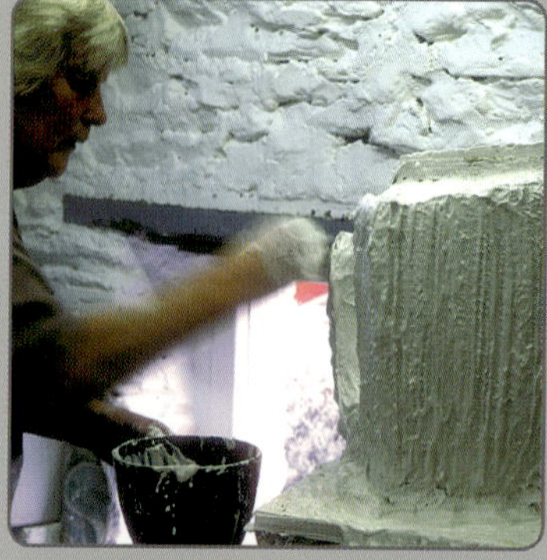
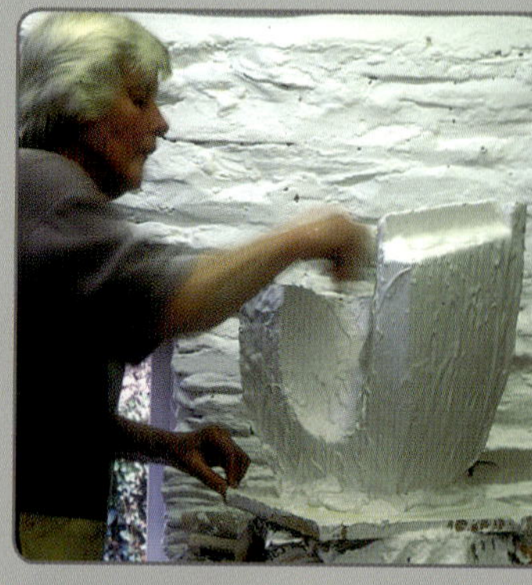
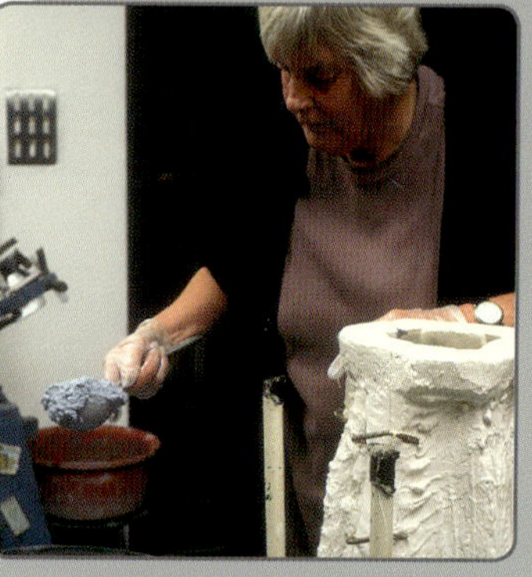
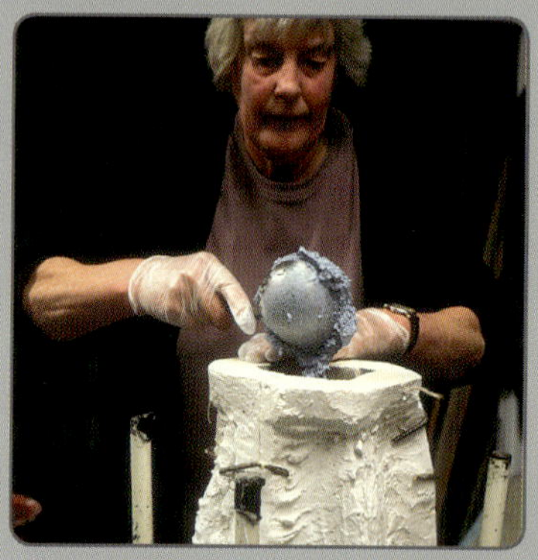
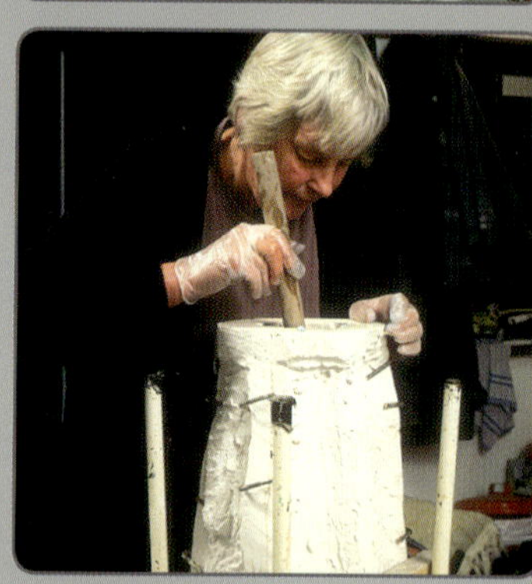

concrete casting

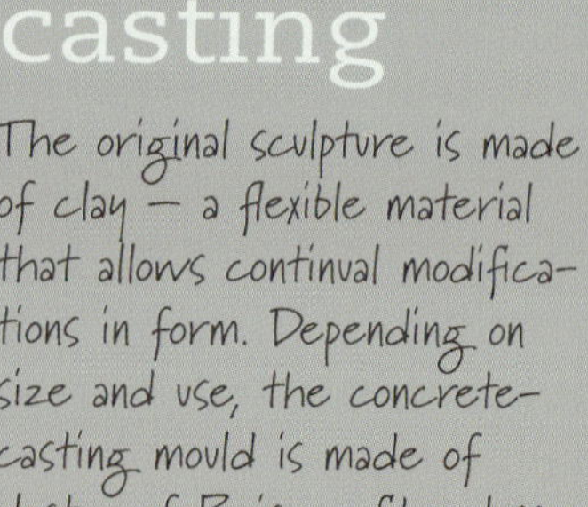
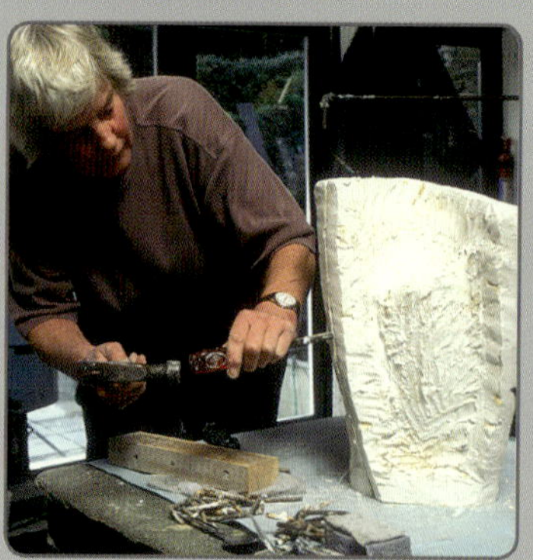
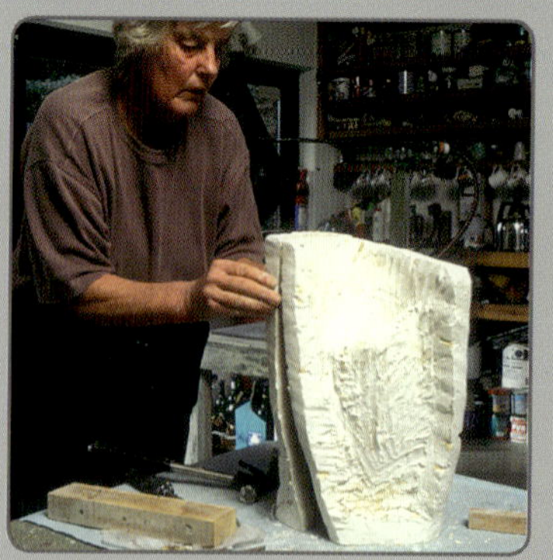
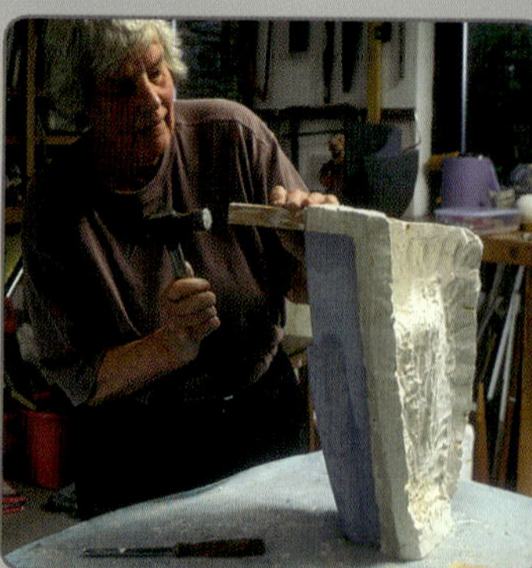

The original sculpture is made of clay – a flexible material that allows continual modifications in form. Depending on size and use, the concrete-casting mould is made of plaster of Paris, or fibreglass. The mould is made in pieces, so that it can be removed cleanly from the clay, and from the finished concrete casting – the skill is in identifying undercuts that could prevent the mould's removal. Brass shims (which can be seen clearly in the top left picture on page 32) define the part lines; the plaster is then applied to the clay, and allowed to set. The mould is cleaned, sealed, waxed and reassembled.

A precise mixture of cement, aggregate, pigment and water make the colour concrete. A slump flow test – filling a container with a known amount of concrete, and measuring its

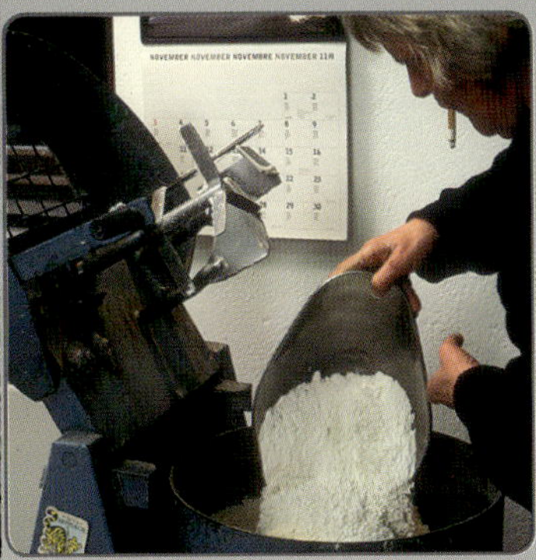

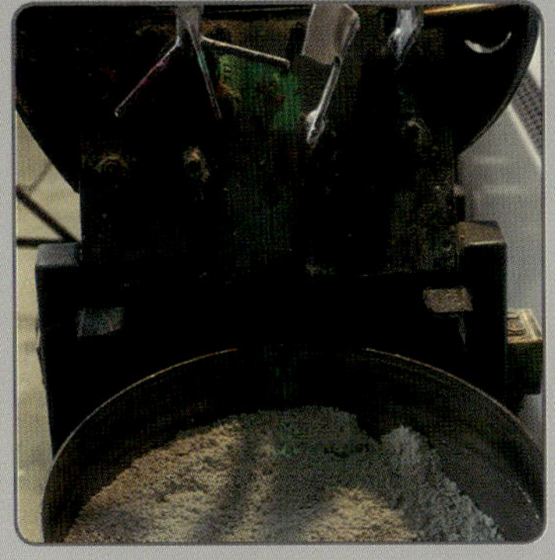

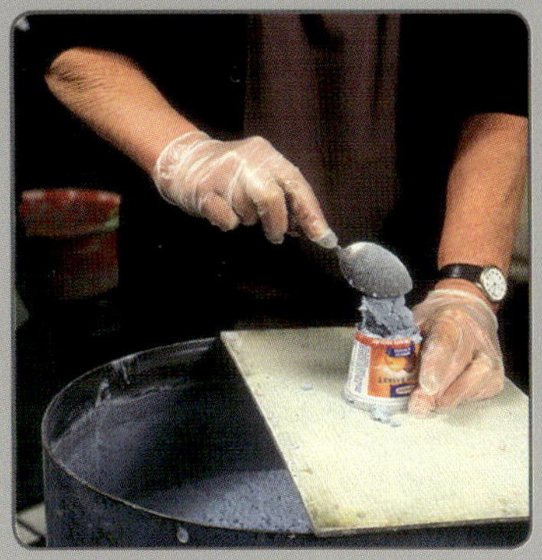

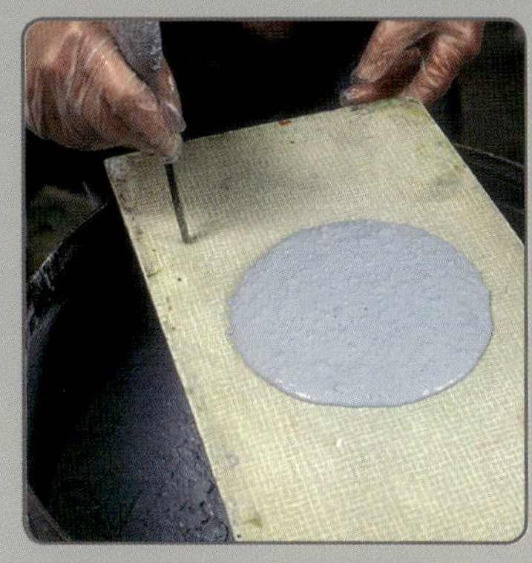

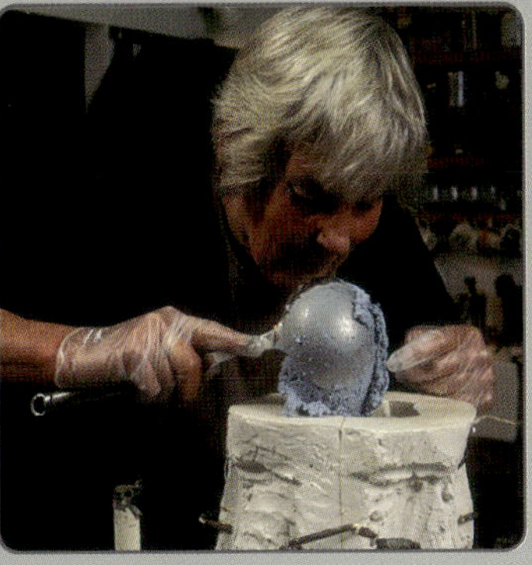

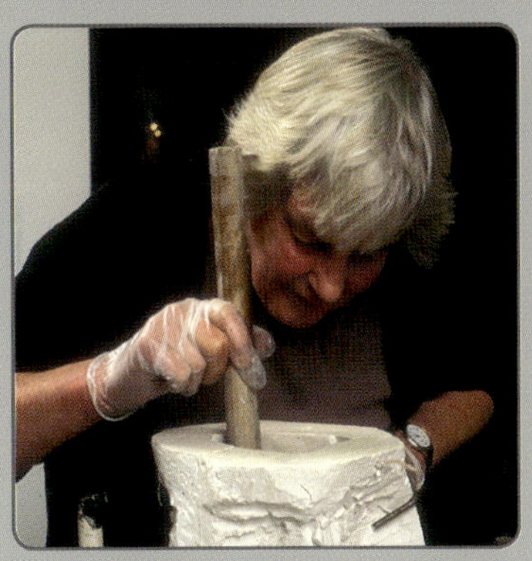

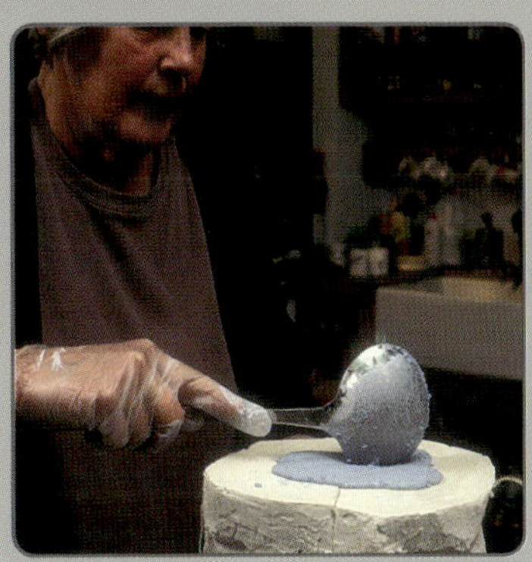

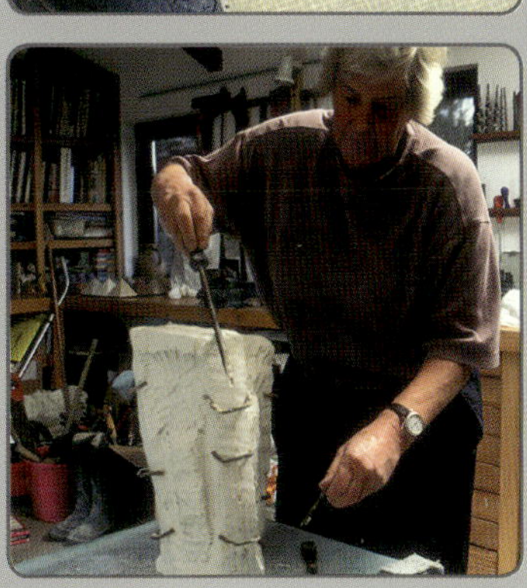

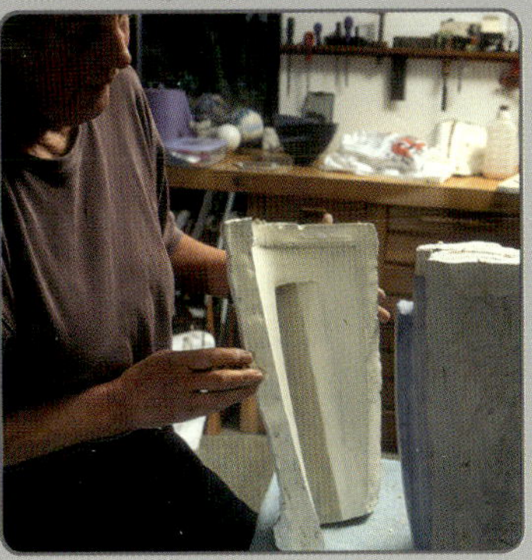

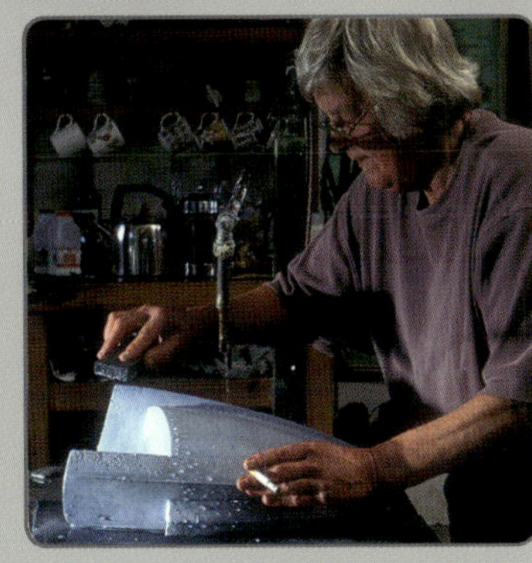

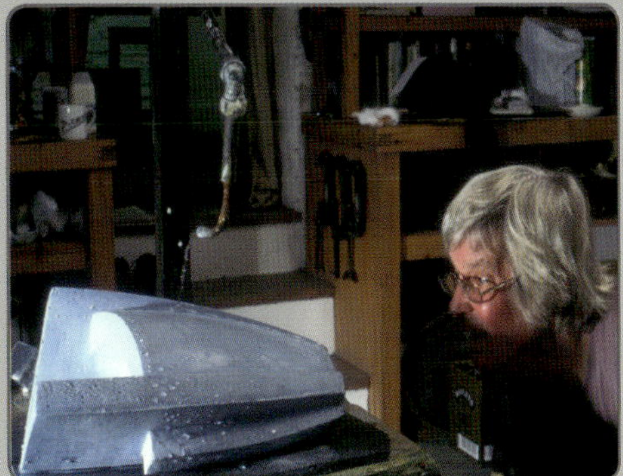

spread – checks consistency of the self-compacting concrete. Casting takes place with the reassembled mould upside down. Concrete is placed in the mould and compacted. When it has set – which takes about 18 hours – the pieces of the mould are separated to reveal the concrete sculpture within.

The final, highly polished surface finish is produced by a laborious process of grinding, grouting, sanding and polishing.

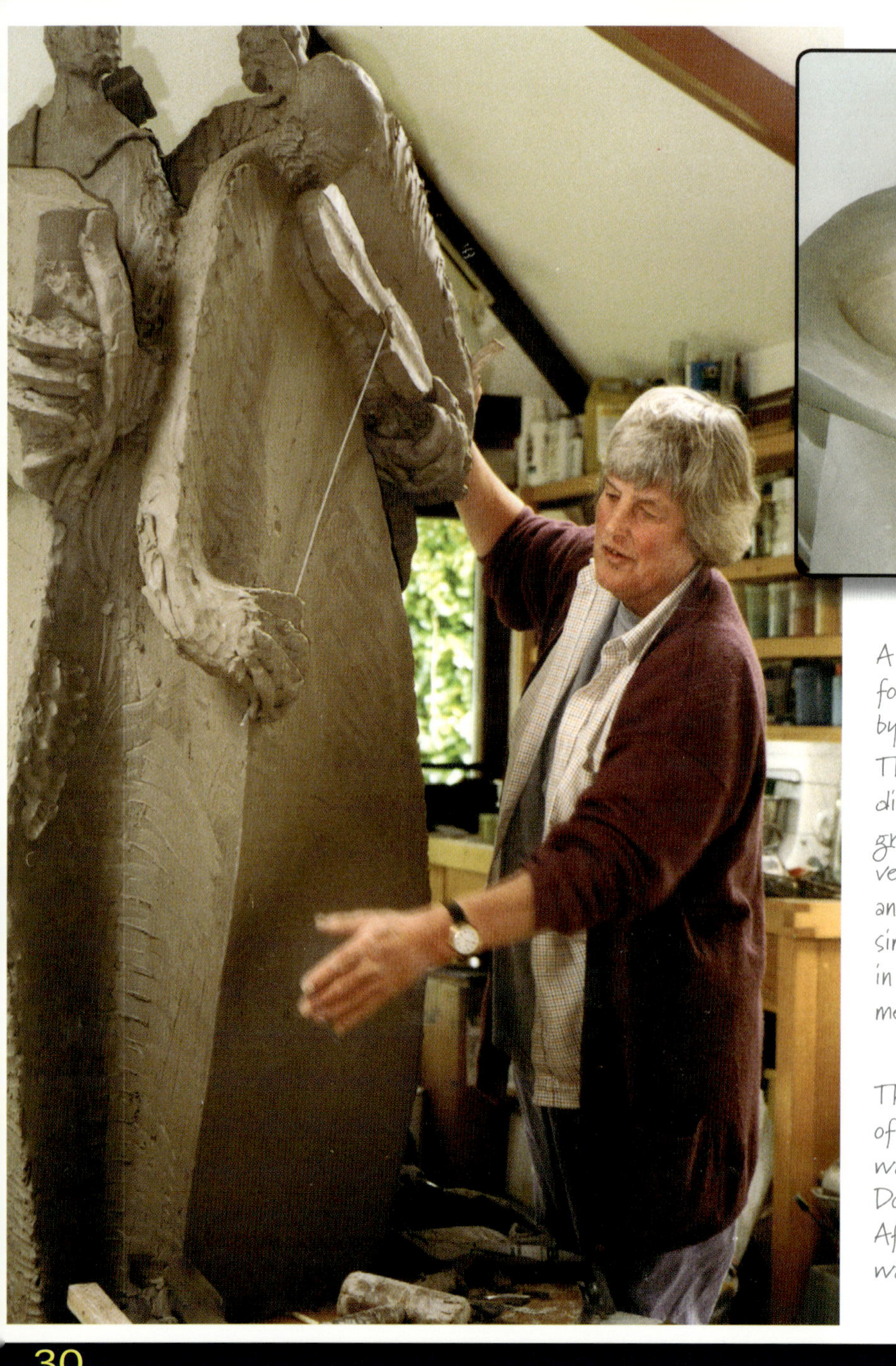

A group of street musicians seemed appropriate for a busy pedestrian area with two pubs close by and a place where buskers often perform. Three musicians, playing banjo, fiddle and accordion, stand back-to-back, forming a circular group 62 inches tall. The legs make a simple vertical rhythm; higher up, instruments, hands and arms make a more intense pattern. The simplification of the figures and the filled-in shapes between them is dictated by the method of producing a sculpture in concrete.

The original sculpture was made of 12cwt of clay, from which a fibreglass piece-mould was taken. A special mix including marble and Doulting stone was designed for Les Jongleurs. After striking the mould, the concrete surface was ground and polished to a terrazzo finish.

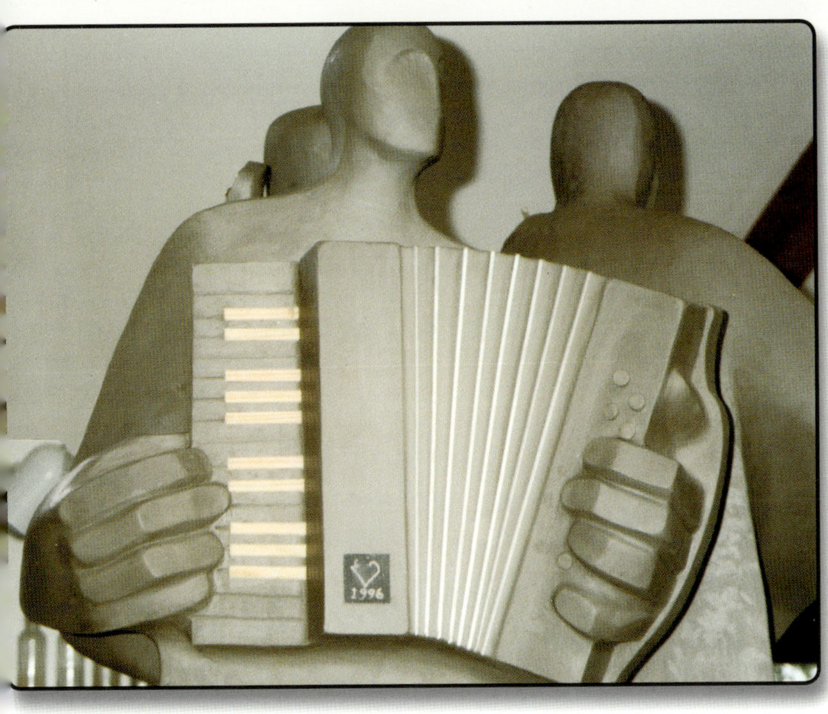

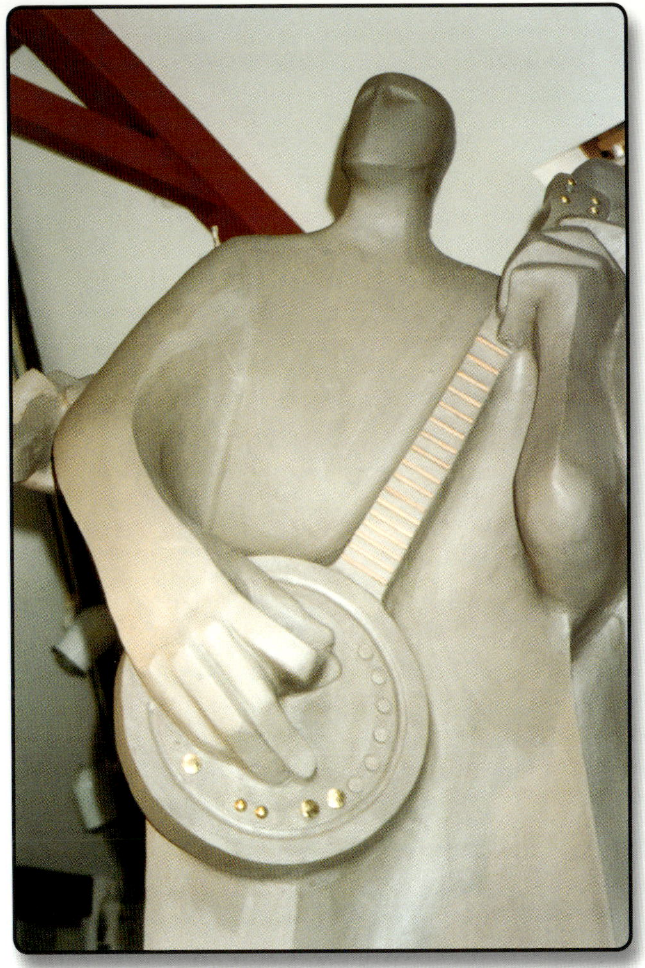

A wood and steel armature supported the 12cwt of clay used to model the figures.

In the early stages, it was a continual struggle to make room for instruments and arms while keeping the centre core as small as possible. There is a fine balance in making the players credible and lively, strong but elegant and not vulnerable, and maintaining an abstract rhythm in form and pattern. Clay is a remarkably flexible material ... and allows modifications in form until the end. When the carved surface relates to the concrete form, the sculpture will be cast.

Les Jongleurs

In 1996, Carole was commissioned by the Jersey Public Sculpture Trust to make a sculpture for Snow Hill Junction, St Helier.

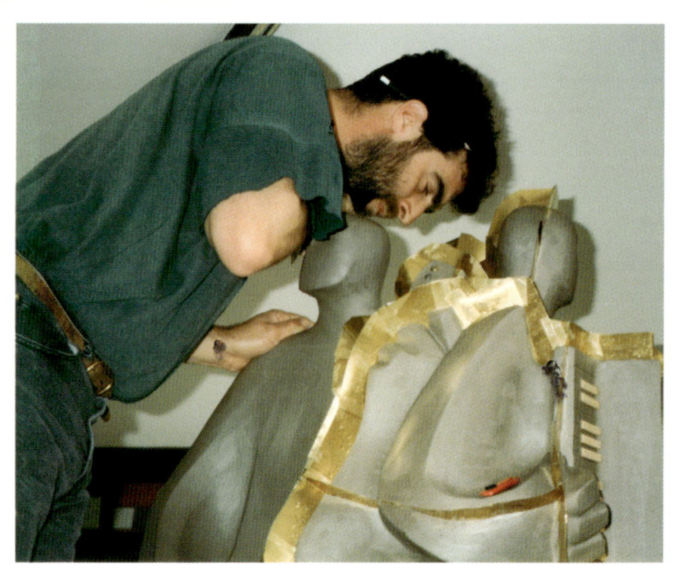

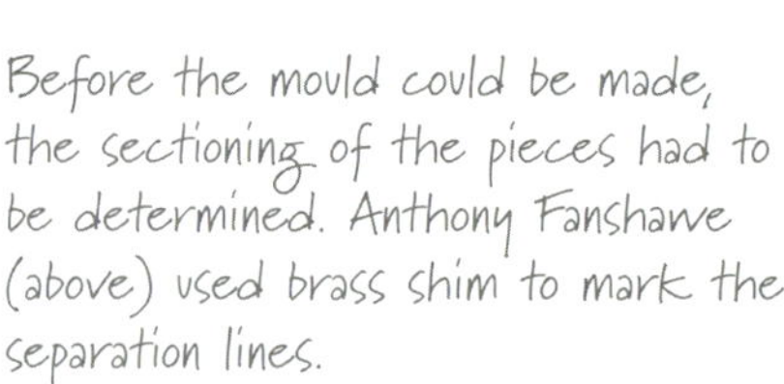

Before the mould could be made, the sectioning of the pieces had to be determined. Anthony Fanshawe (above) used brass shim to mark the separation lines.

Norman Staple (right) made the fibreglass mould.

Thirteen 50kg batches of aggregate, white cement, synthetic fibre, water and plasticiser were carefully weighed ready for a continuous process of mixing in the concrete mixer ... casting was slow at the start – heads with steel reinforcement had to be filled with care; hands and instruments took a long time to fill properly. Further up the shape made it easier, but a very big space to fill and to compact. It took eight hours from start to finish.

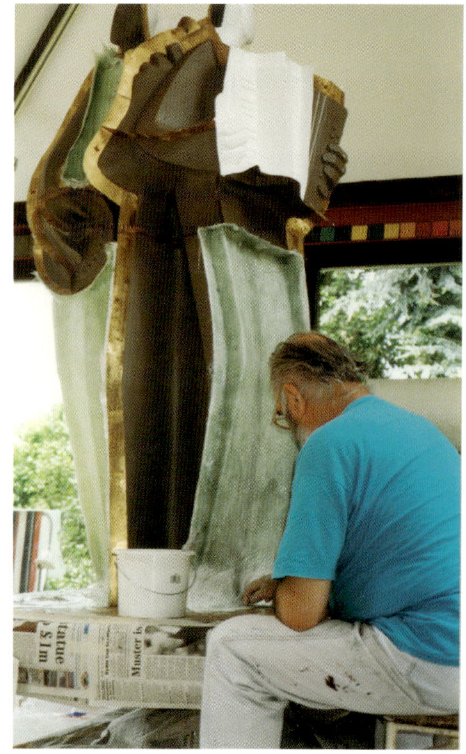

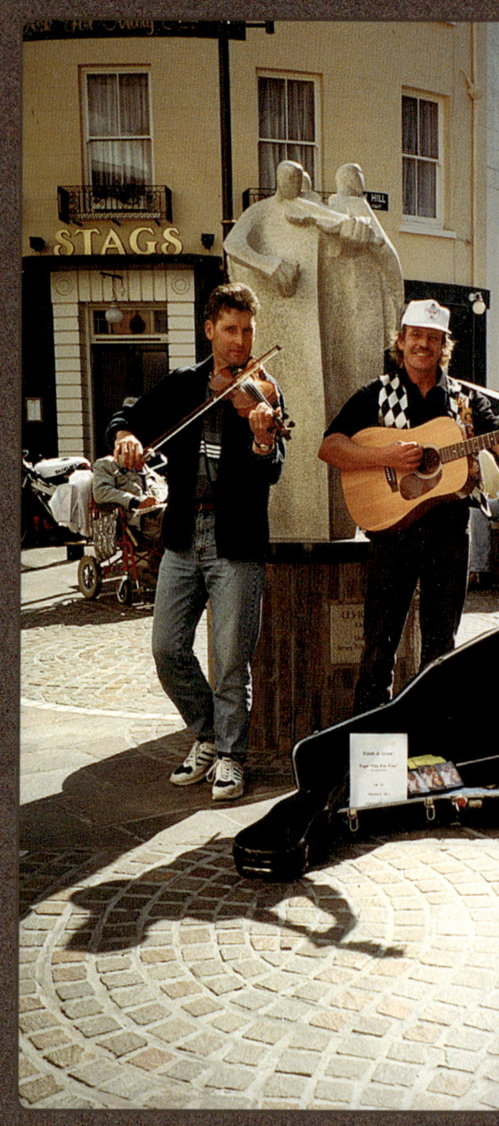

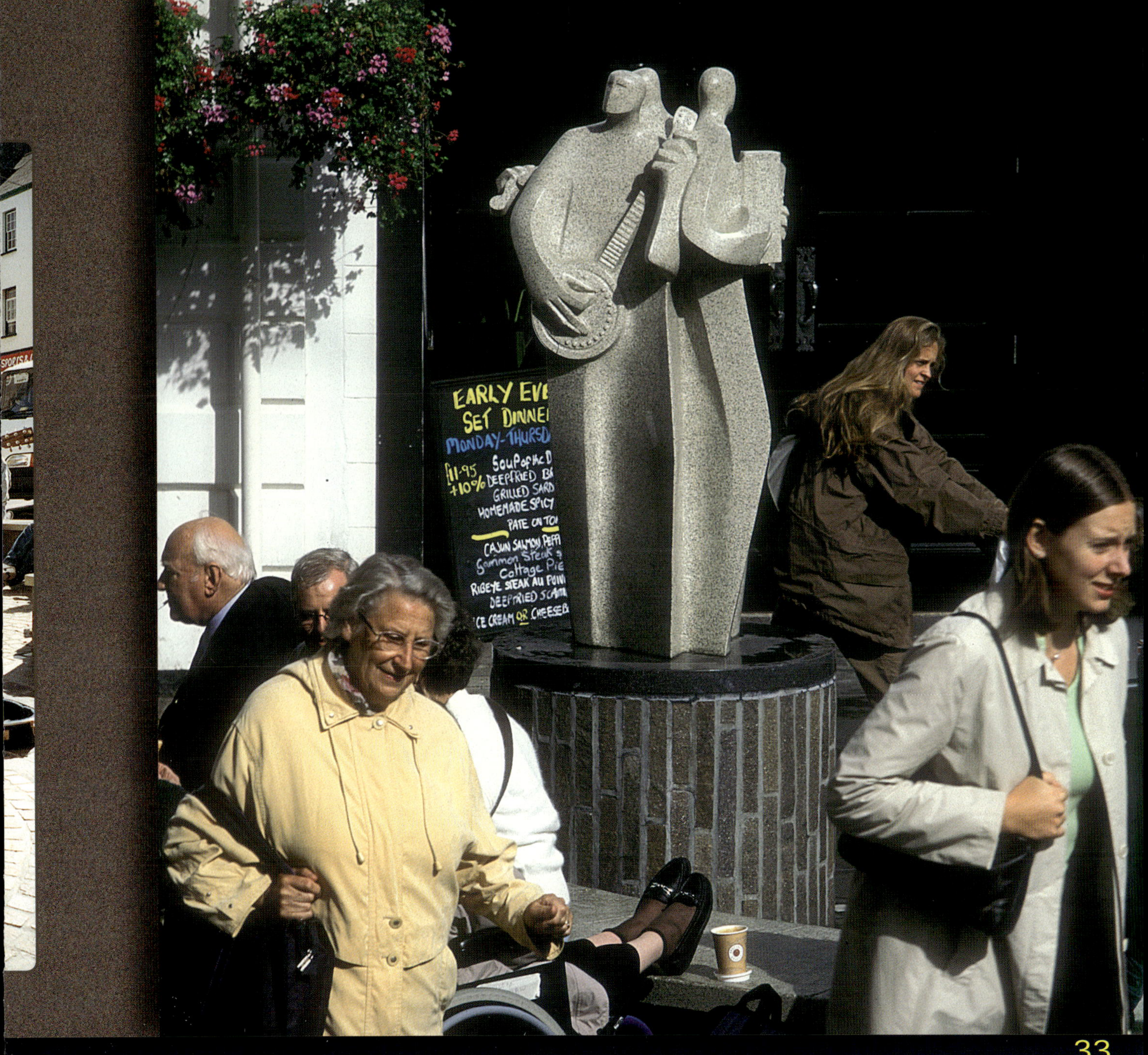
EARLY EVE
SET DINNE
MONDAY-THURSD
£11.95
+10%
GRILLED SARD
HOMEMADE SPICY
Cottage Pie
ICE CREAM OR CHEESEB

the Red Carpet

The home of the Edinburgh International Festival is the Edinburgh Festival Centre – built in the mid-19th century to the grand designs of James Gillespie Graham and Augustus Welby Pugin, as the Assembly Hall and offices of the Church of Scotland. The building was transformed in the 1990s by Benjamin Tindall Architects, who wanted to 'roll out the red carpet' for all visitors. The Edinburgh Festival Society commissioned Carole Vincent to design the carpet, and Anthony Fanshawe to make it in brightly coloured concrete paving.

The Red Carpet is a diagonal tessellation of 300mm squares, bordered by squares, triangles and half-squares, with three reds dominating the rich tapestry of nine colours. 10m long and 5m wide, it is laid at the entrance to the Hub, between the pavement and the front door. Over 500 tiles weigh nearly 4 tons!

First thoughts were random colour and random tessellation – nice idea but not practical! To manufacture in concrete a simple tessellation would be preferable. This at 1 square per 12 inch slab gave me some idea of the scale. I realize now many of the colours were not right for a 19th-century building.

I now think the diagonal format will be much livelier. I need to make colour samples in concrete – the aggregate will reduce the impact of these colours.

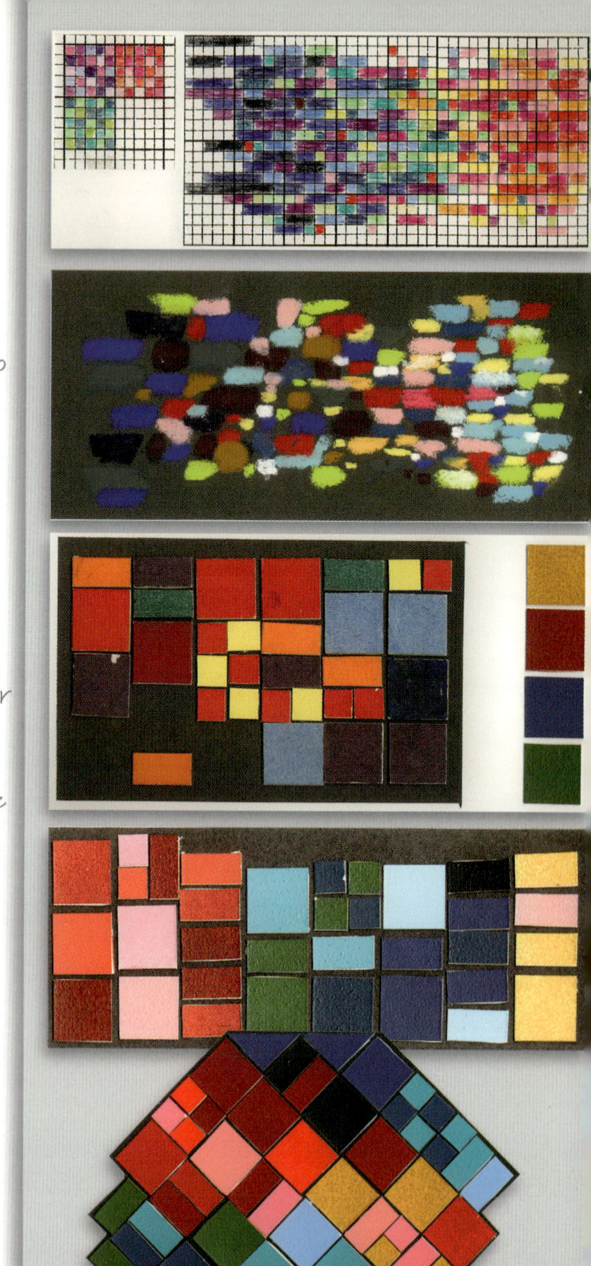

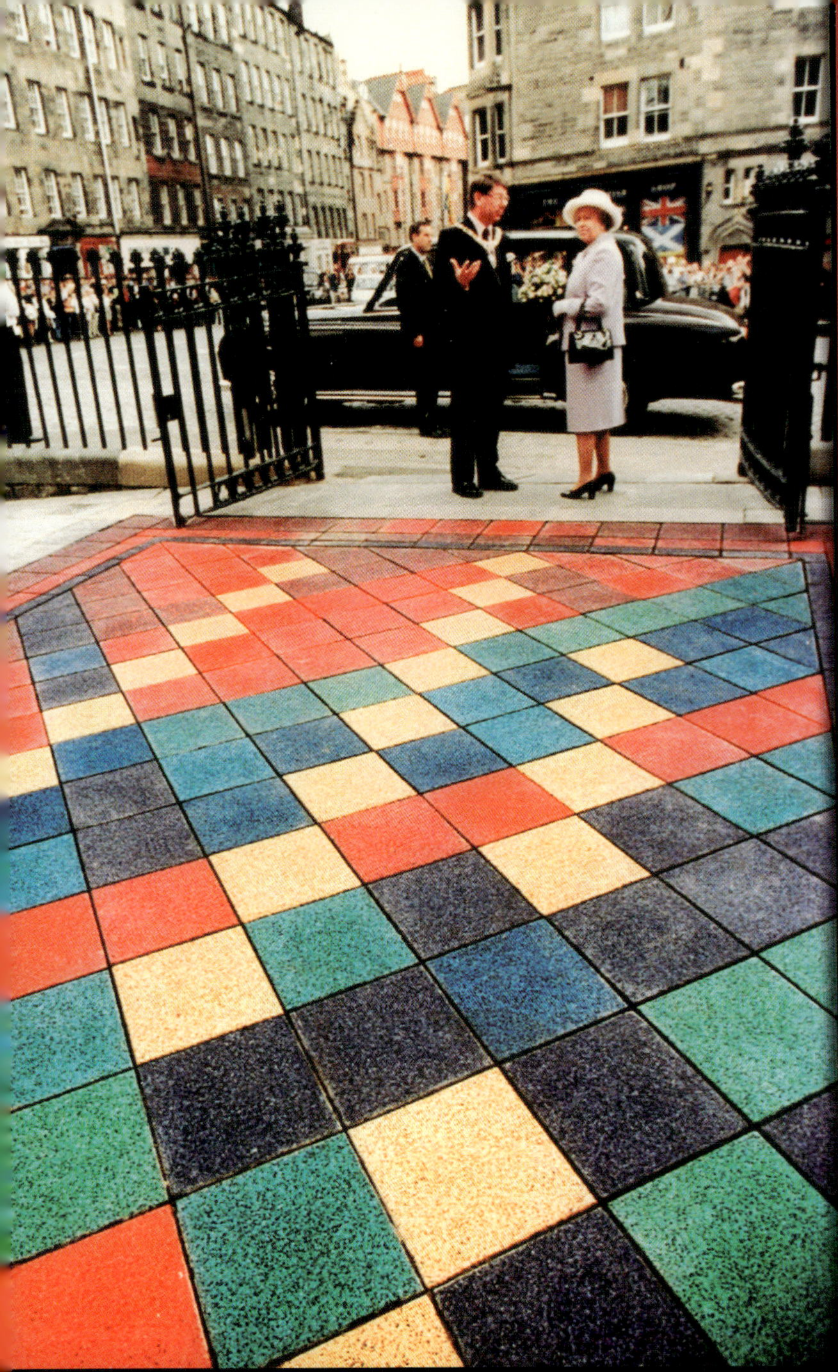

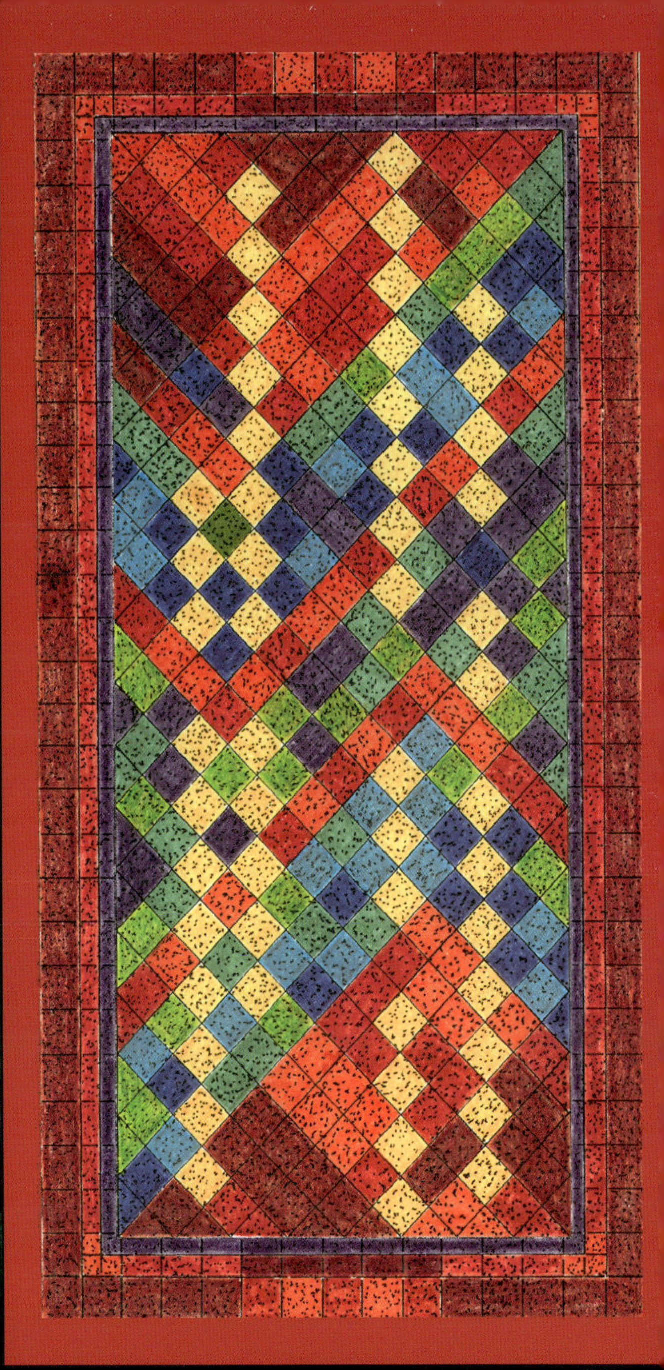

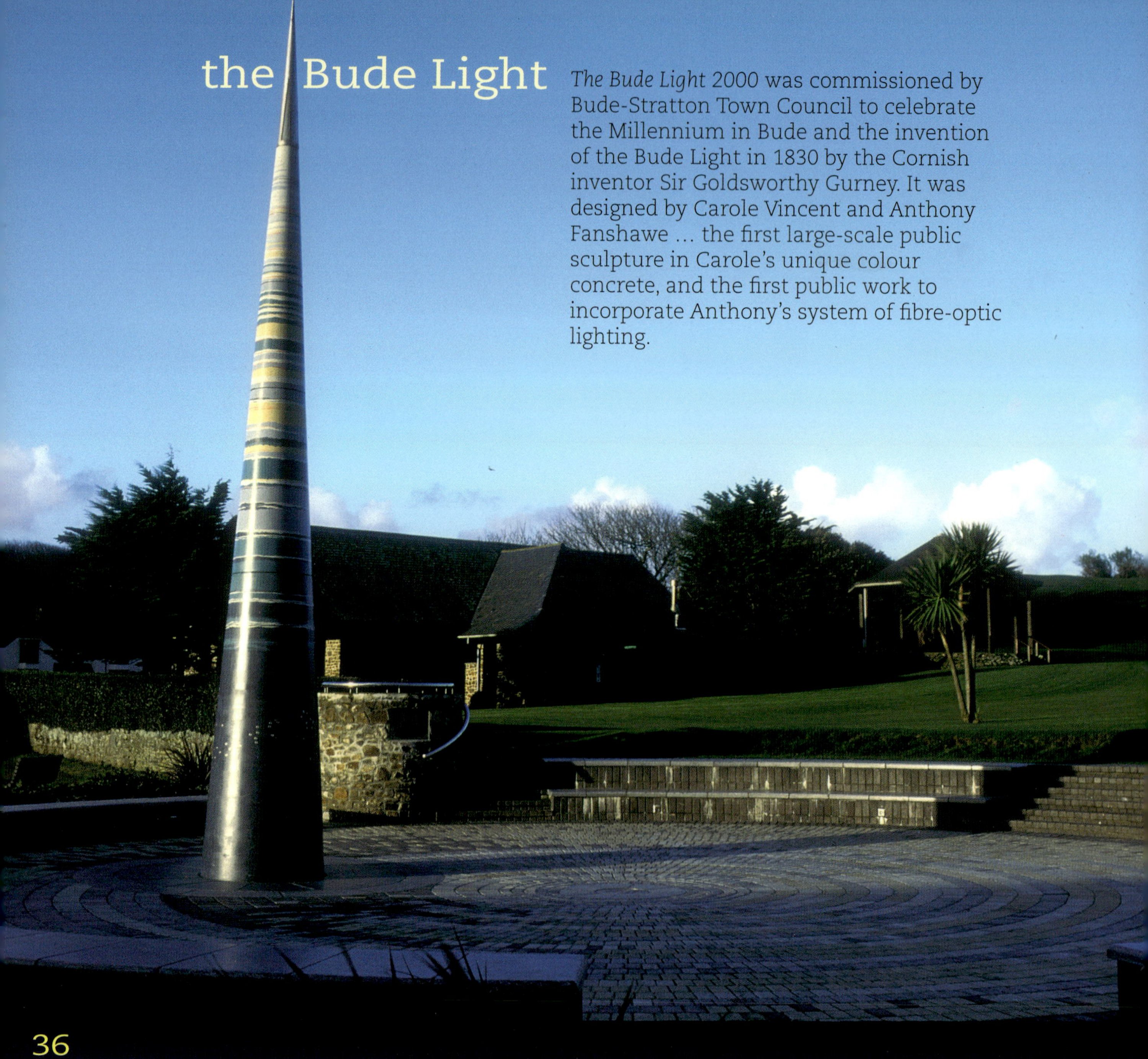

the Bude Light

The Bude Light 2000 was commissioned by Bude-Stratton Town Council to celebrate the Millennium in Bude and the invention of the Bude Light in 1830 by the Cornish inventor Sir Goldsworthy Gurney. It was designed by Carole Vincent and Anthony Fanshawe … the first large-scale public sculpture in Carole's unique colour concrete, and the first public work to incorporate Anthony's system of fibre-optic lighting.

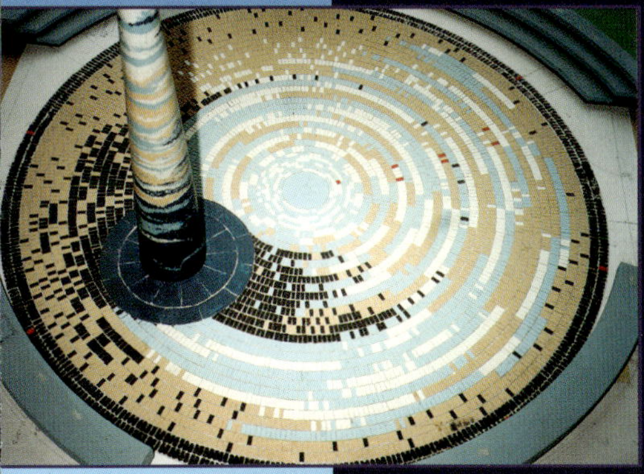

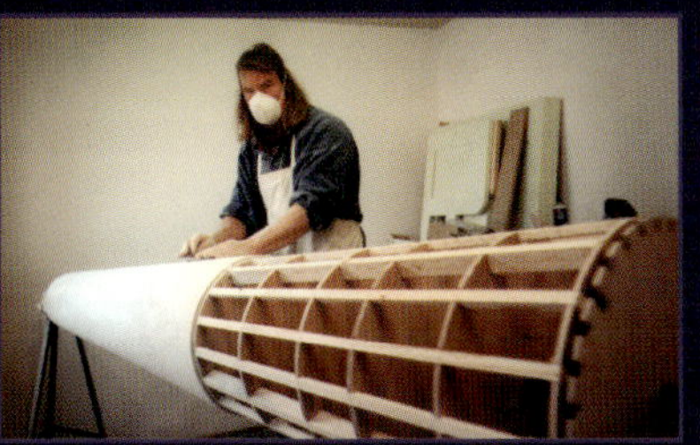

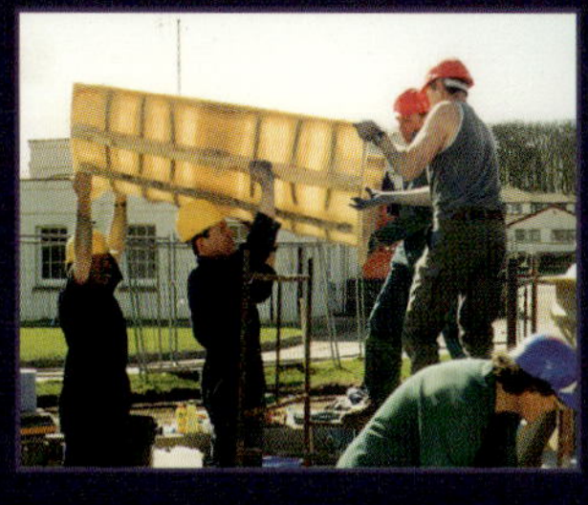

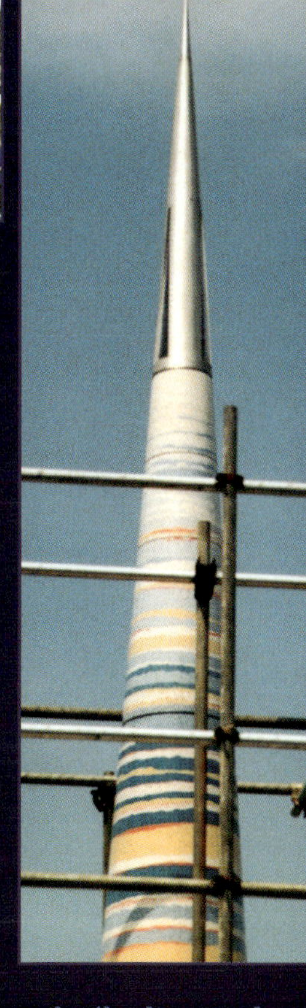

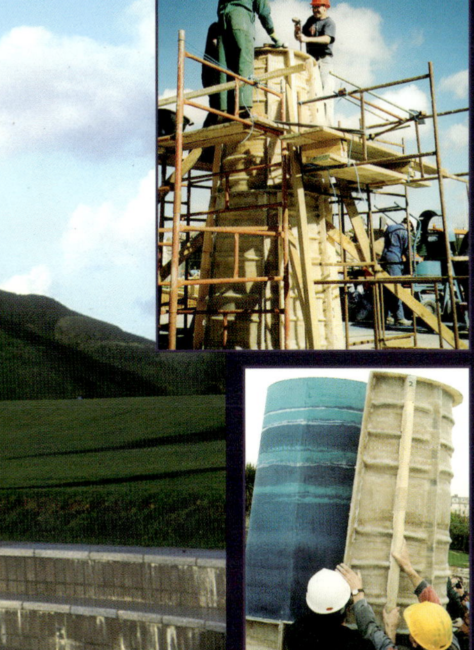

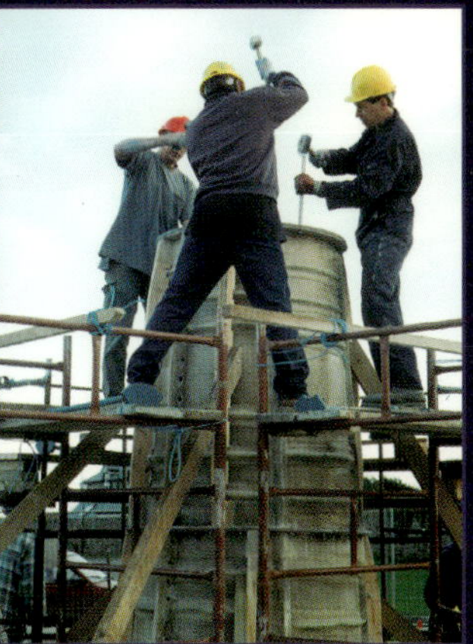

height: 9m
base diameter: 1.2m
weight: 6 tonnes ...
in concrete the colours of sand, sea and sky, topped by a 1.8m stainless-steel lantern containing three fibre-optic lenses. In the dark blue concrete near the base, lights reflect the constellations on 17 May 2000, when there was a rare close proximity of the classical planets.

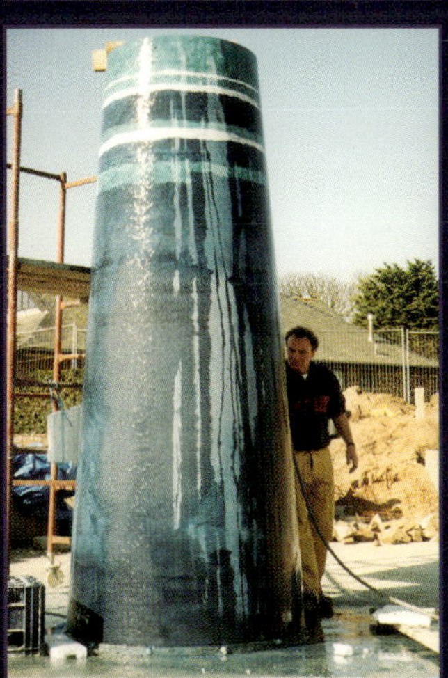

Sir Goldsworthy Gurney built the castle, which is behind the *Bude Light 2000*. He lit it by injecting a stream of oxygen into an oil flame, and reflecting the light through the rooms. He went on to light the House of Commons with three Bude Lights – replacing 280 candles! He adapted his light for lighthouses, creating flashing beams and the intermittent-sequence signalling system, which was patented in 1839.

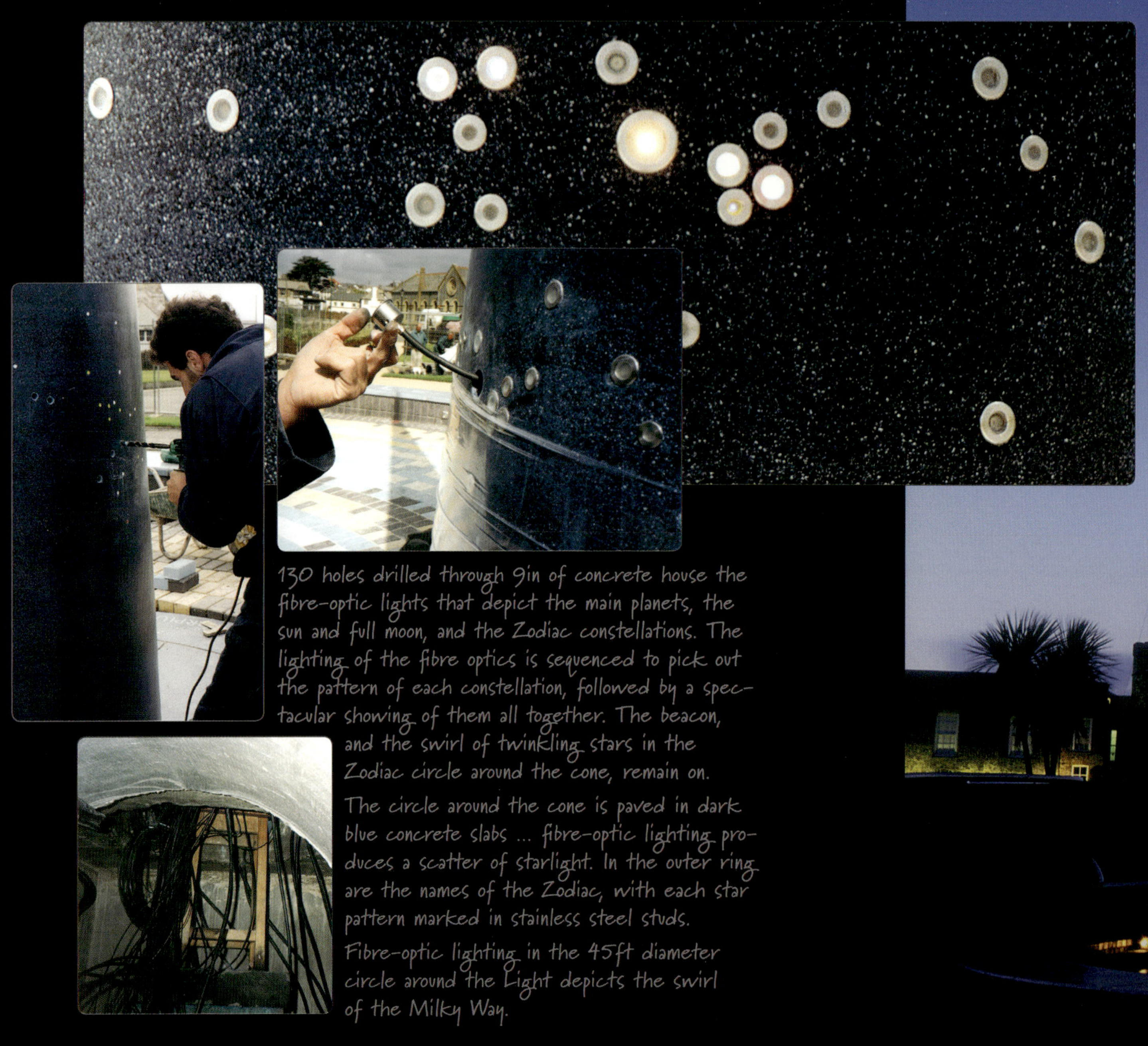

130 holes drilled through 9in of concrete house the fibre-optic lights that depict the main planets, the sun and full moon, and the Zodiac constellations. The lighting of the fibre optics is sequenced to pick out the pattern of each constellation, followed by a spectacular showing of them all together. The beacon, and the swirl of twinkling stars in the Zodiac circle around the cone, remain on.

The circle around the cone is paved in dark blue concrete slabs ... fibre-optic lighting produces a scatter of starlight. In the outer ring are the names of the Zodiac, with each star pattern marked in stainless steel studs.

Fibre-optic lighting in the 45ft diameter circle around the Light depicts the swirl of the Milky Way.

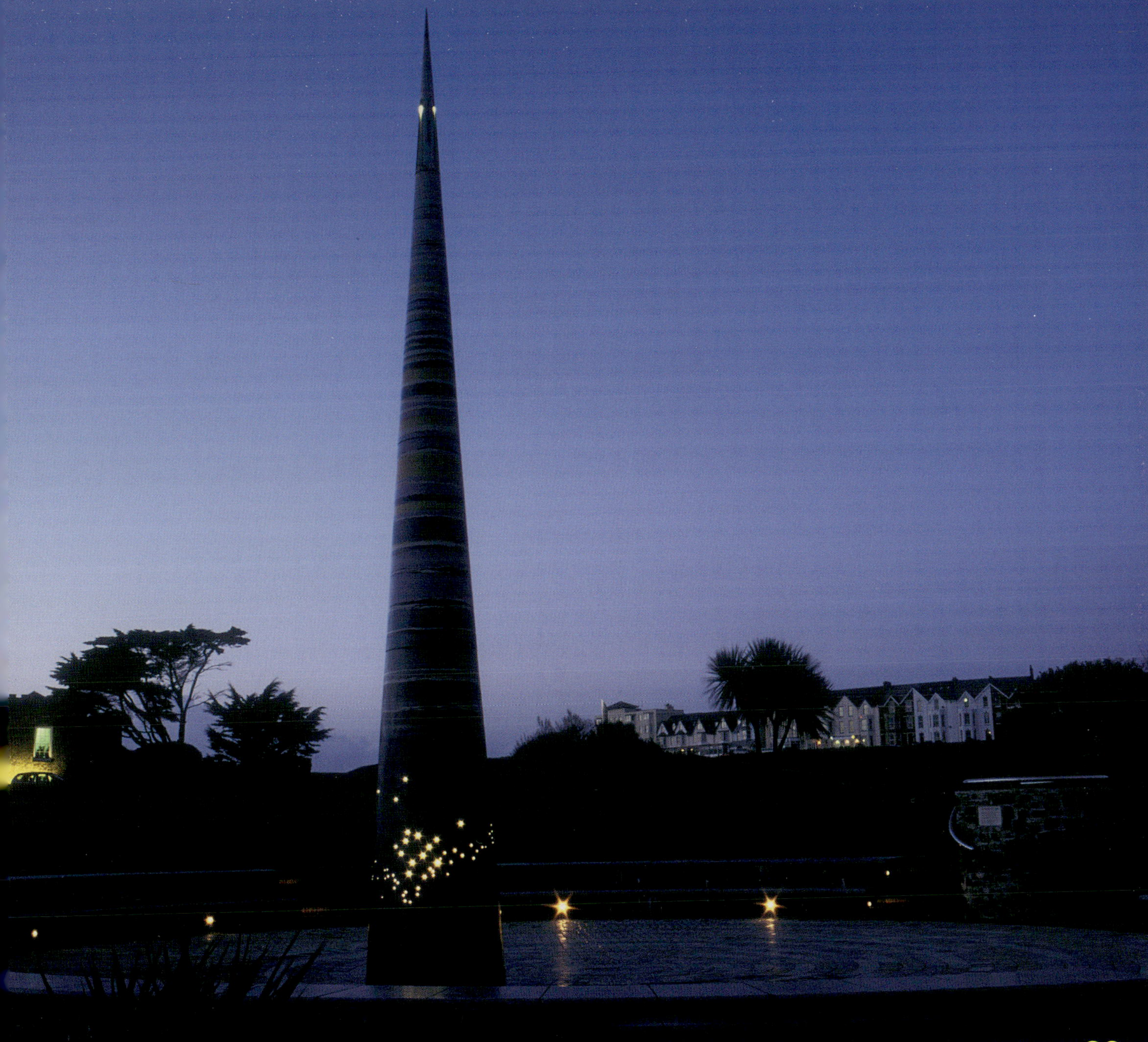

the Blue Circle Garden

In 2001, Carole fulfilled a 40-year ambition to have a show garden at the Royal Horticultural Society's Chelsea Flower Show. Blue Circle Industries plc sponsored her to take her colour concrete garden at Half Acre to Chelsea.

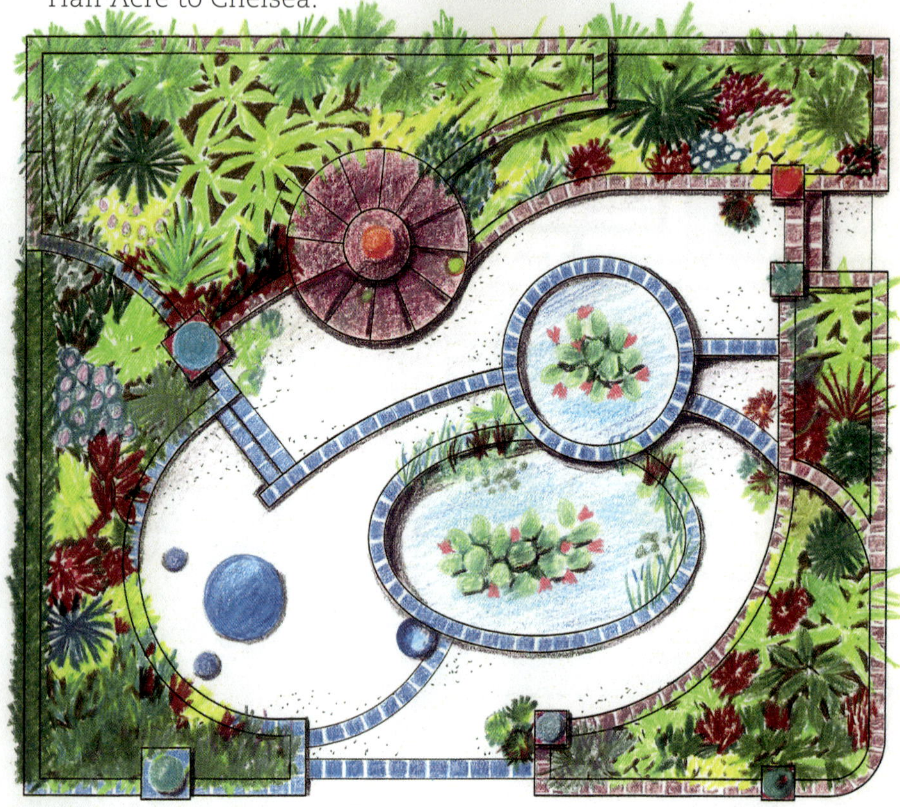

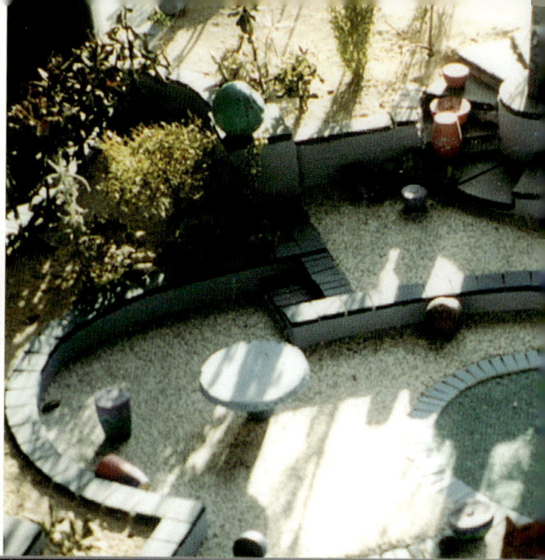

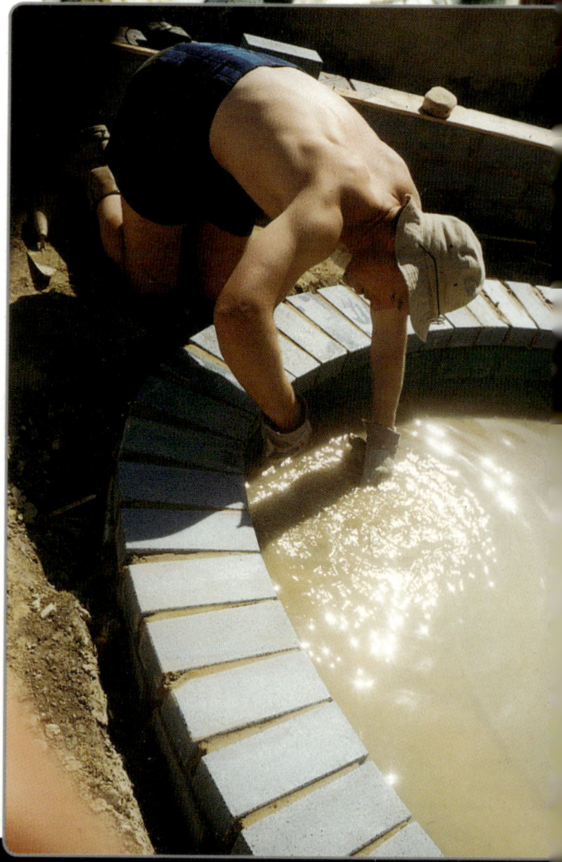

Six tonnes of colour concrete were cast ... as pots, cones, bricks, slabs and steps. It took 19 days and 16 wood moulds to produce 300 bricks; 25 days and 12 moulds to produce 300 coping slabs.

Two ponds were produced in fibreglass. Their similarity in shape and colour to mine in concrete was incredible.

Estimates were made for the materials needed for construction: over 1,000 thermalite blocks, 5 tonnes of sand, cement and lime, granite chippings for the paths, and composted bark for the flowerbeds. Also needed were a concrete mixer, generator, stone-cutter and pallet truck – plus a wide range of smaller building tools.

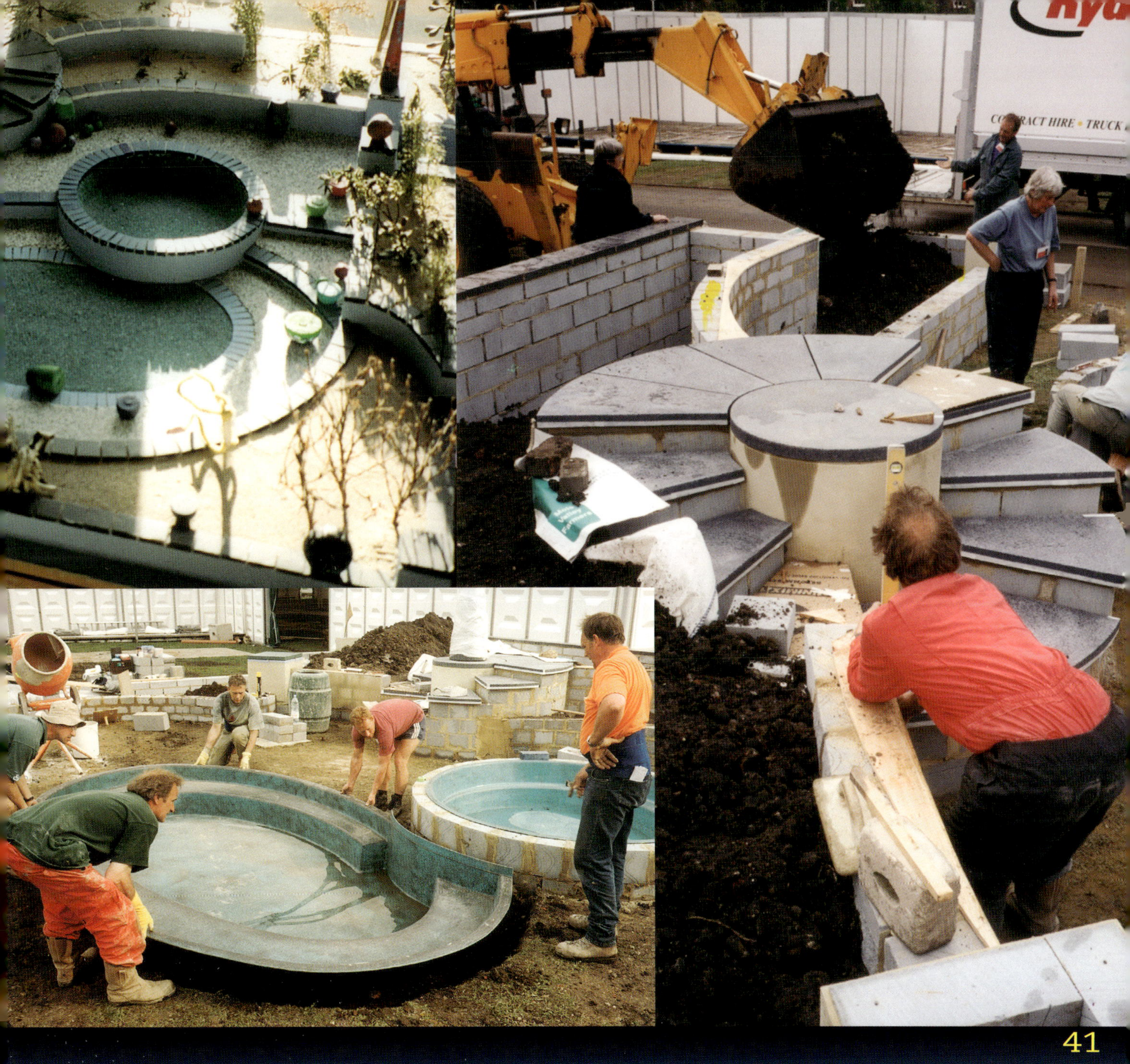

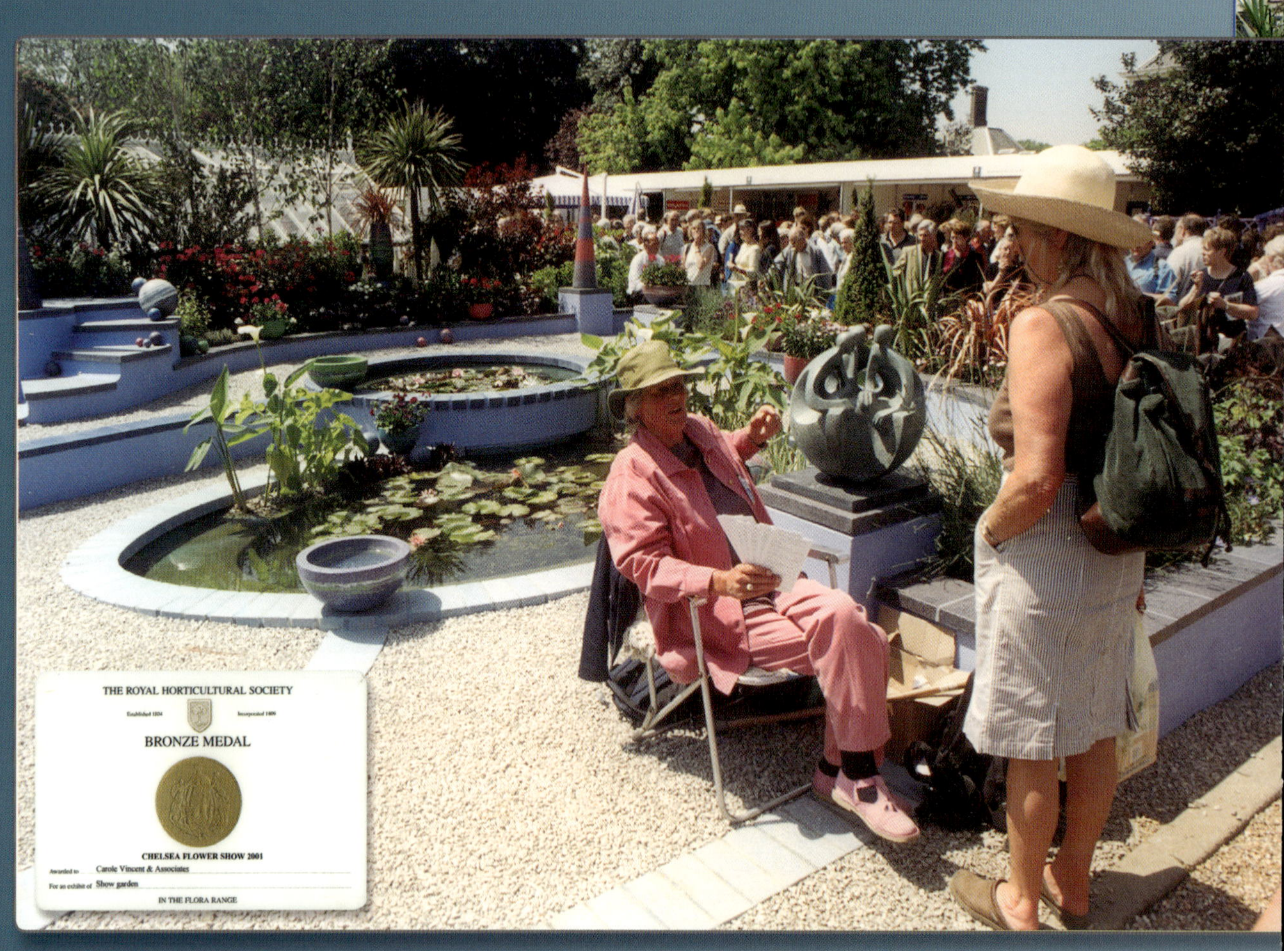
THE ROYAL HORTICULTURAL SOCIETY
BRONZE MEDAL
CHELSEA FLOWER SHOW 2001
Awarded to Carole Vincent & Associates
For an exhibit of Show garden
IN THE FLORA RANGE

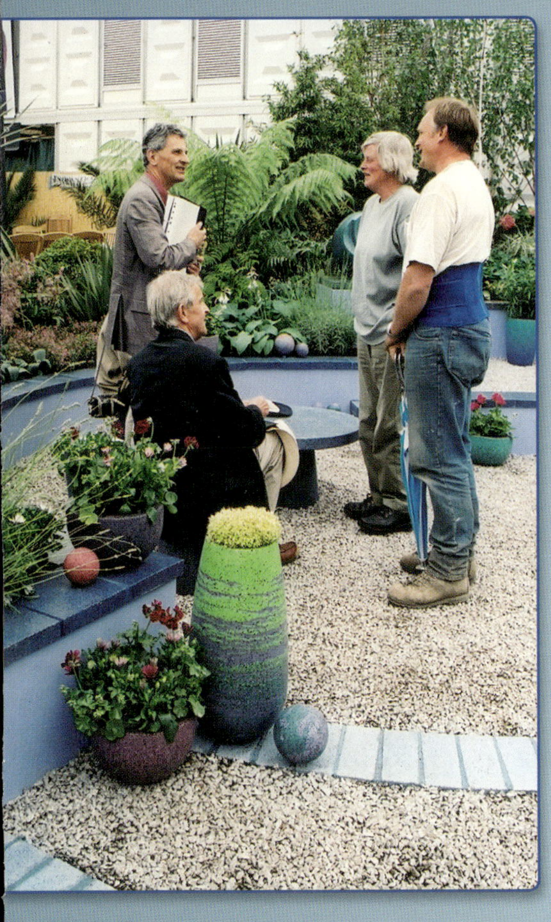

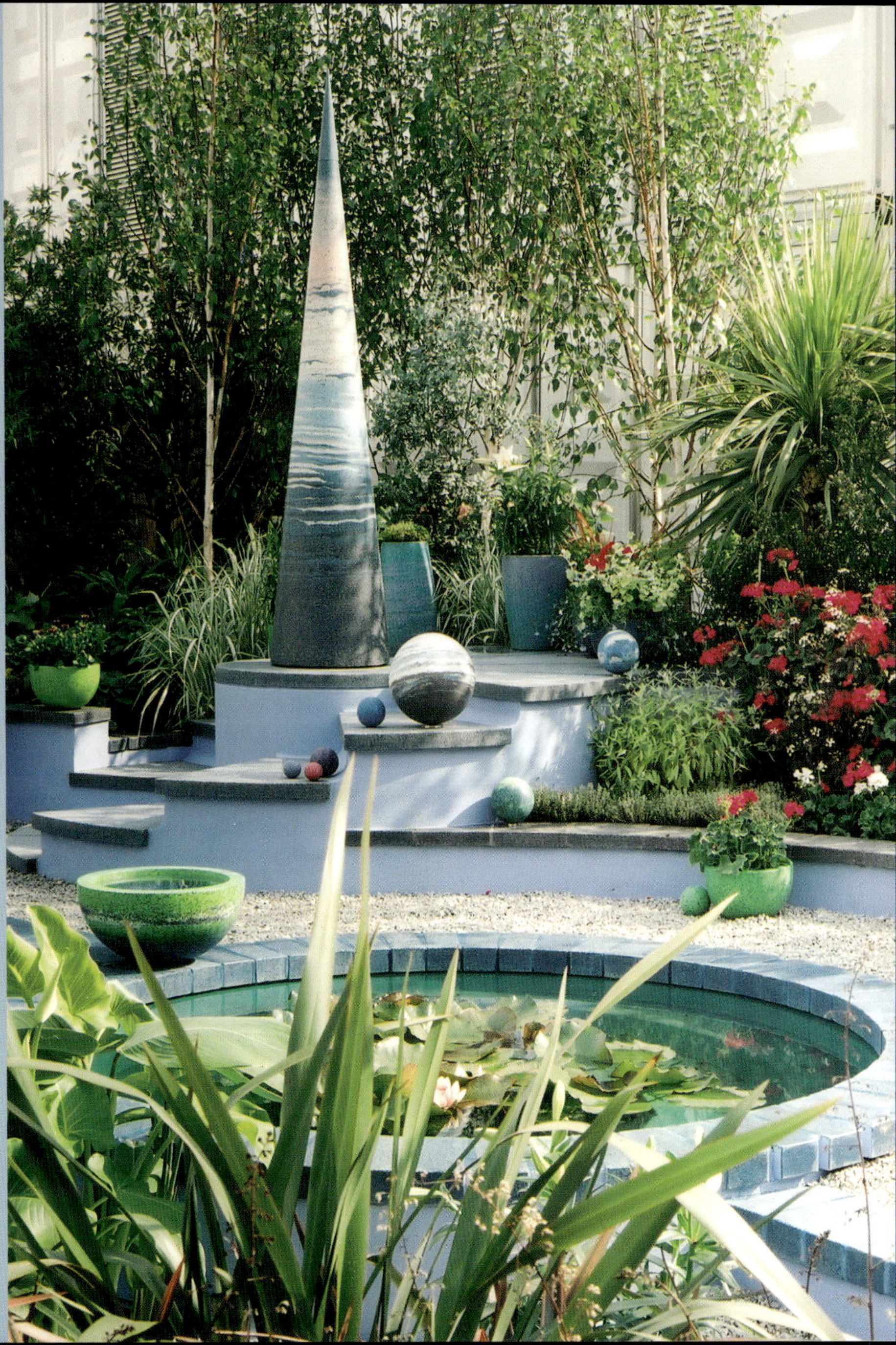

The ambiguous association of a cityscape and a dense forest ... Concrete Jungle explodes two widely held concepts: that concrete is grey and drab, and that urban planting is regimented and unimaginative. The design has the simple formality of a city garden, whose classical structure is complemented by naturalistic planting. The divisions of the square space are based on the Golden Section, and emphasize the power of the diagonal in the design of levels and pathways. A series of square, shallow ponds diagonally set rise one above the other in diminishing sizes conforming to the Fibonacci series: 1:1:2:3:5:8. Water flows from one to the next.

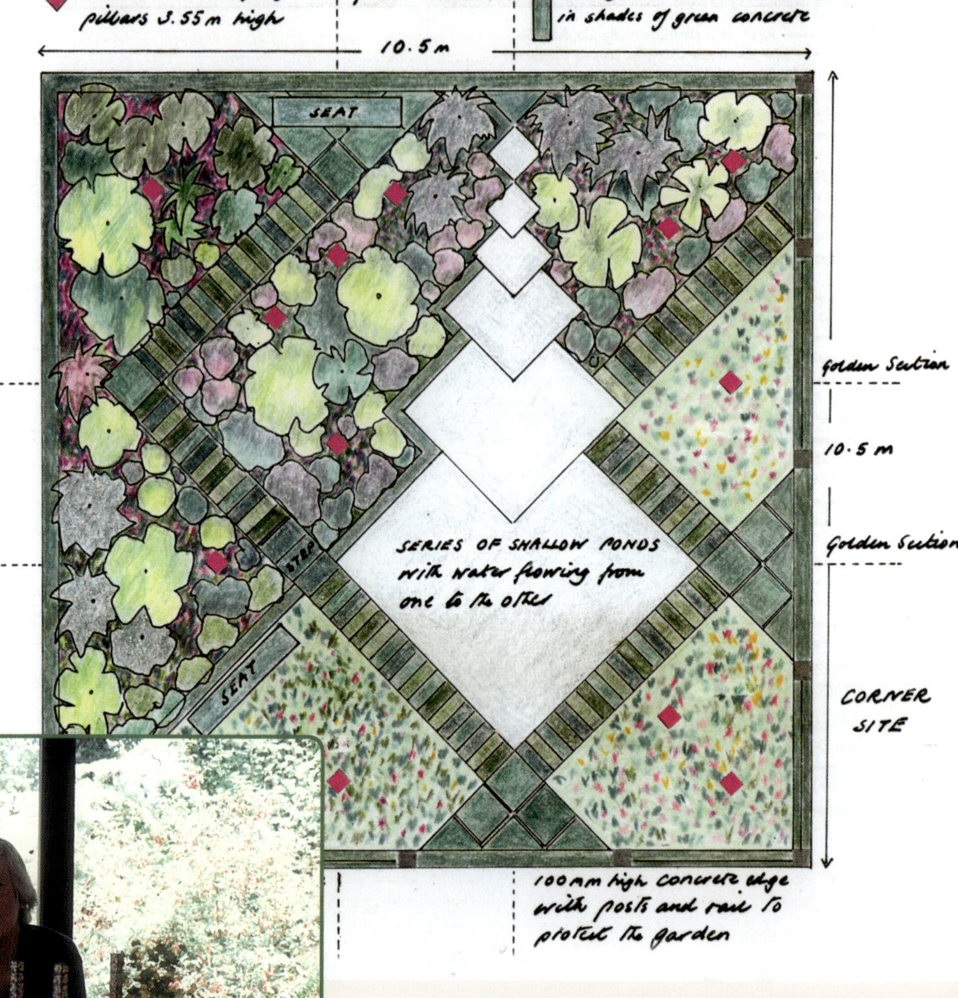

Twelve slender pillars of highly polished colour concrete form a camouflage of greens, with flashes of orange, pink and purple, which disguises the columns' formal structure and provides colour in the upper storey of plants. Each pillar is cast in sections related to the Fibonacci series – further establishing the

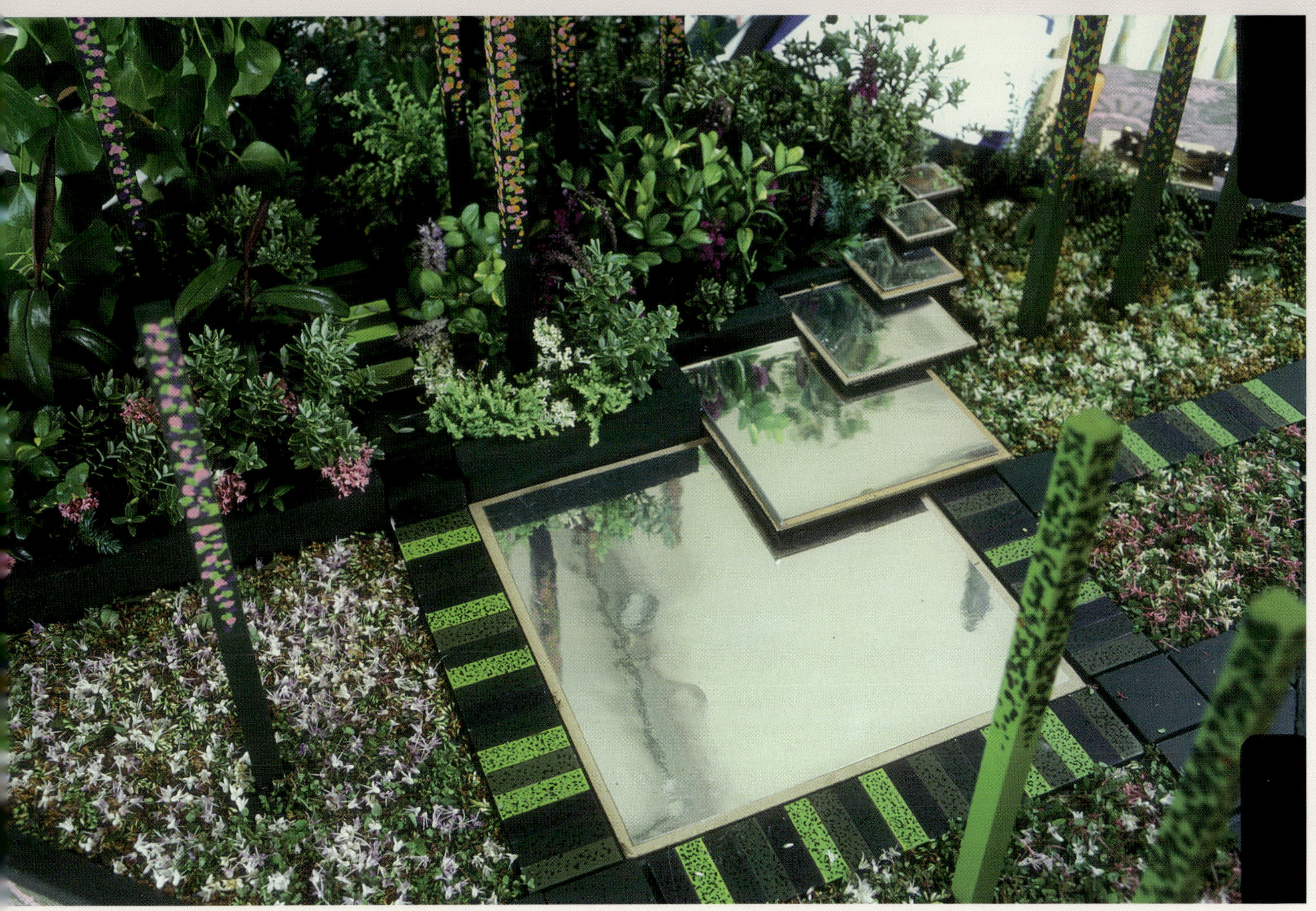

connection with plants, whose growth patterns naturally conform to the series. The colour in the concrete is integral and exploits a new method of mixing. Self-compacting concrete allows different colours to flow in fluid patches, while retaining crisp edges.

Concrete Jungle
work in progress

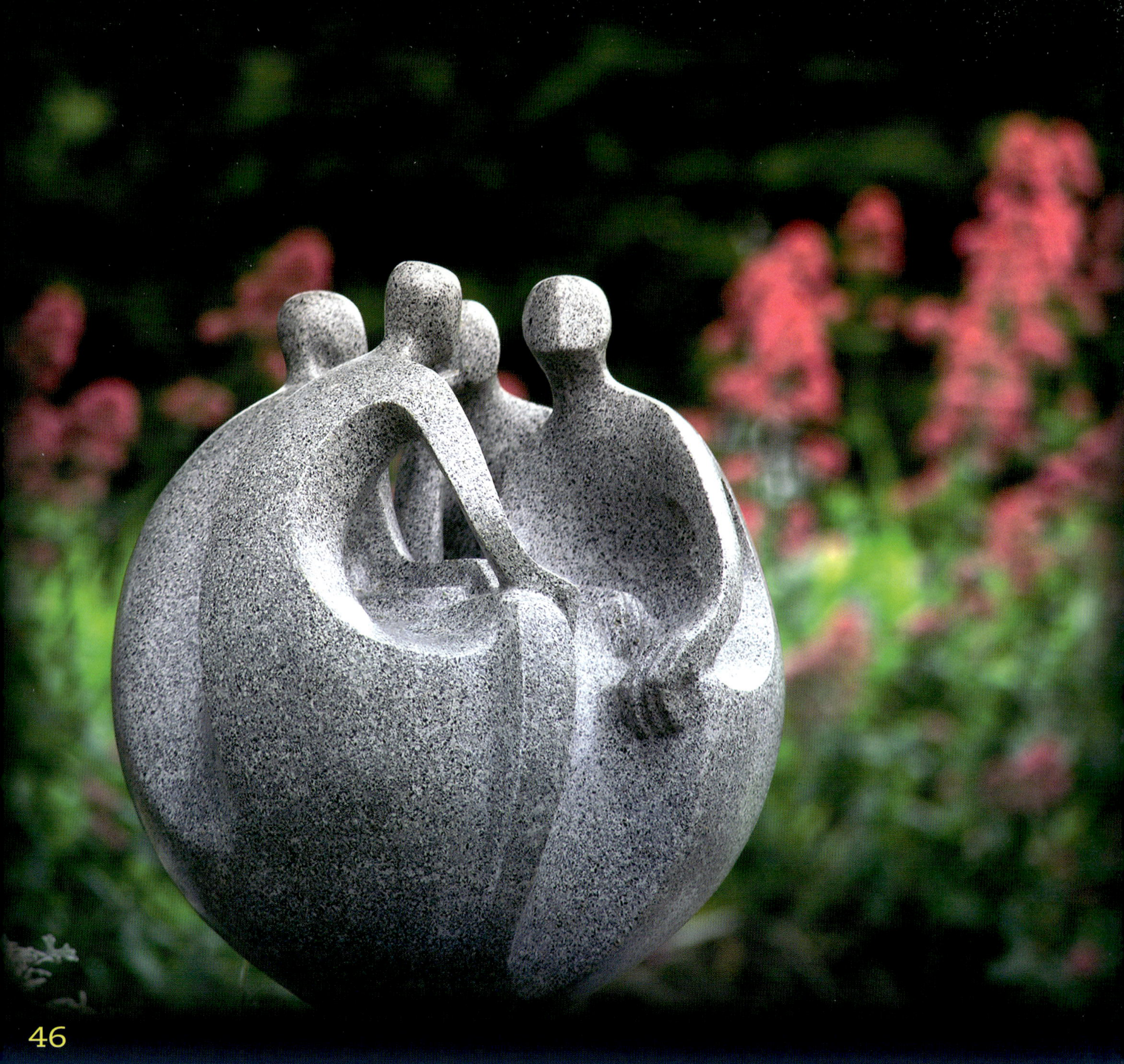

smaller work

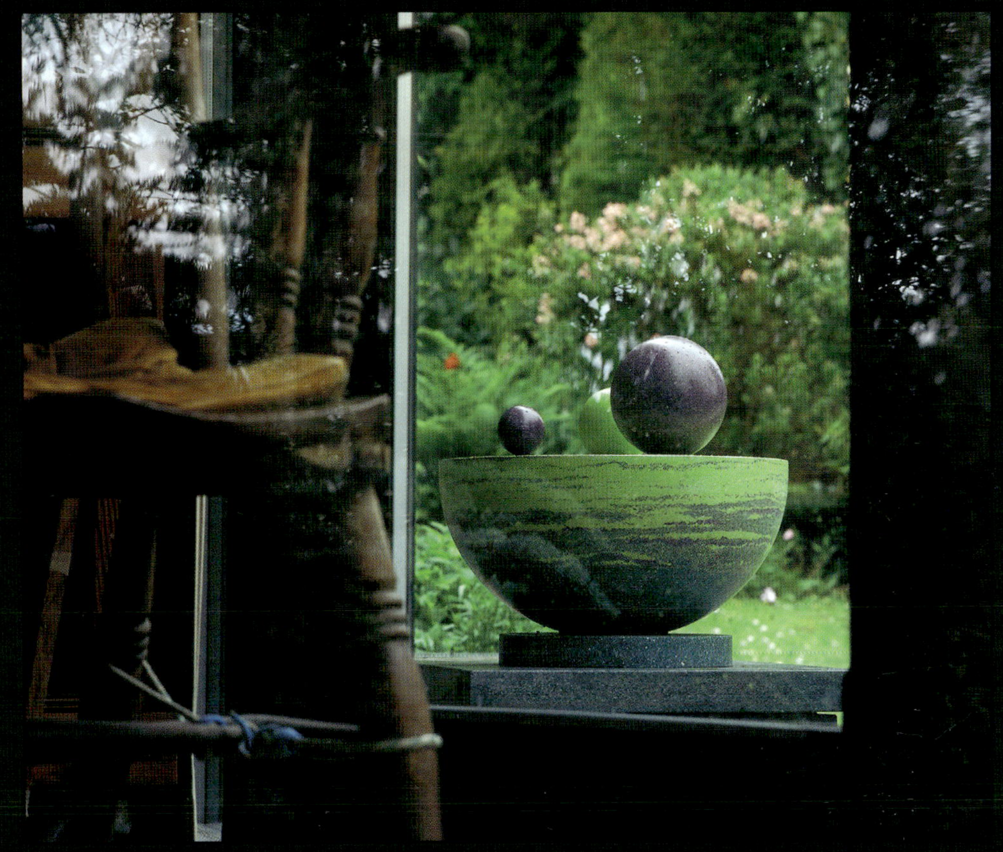

Green Pond, 1995, is one of a series of still-life sculptures in colour concrete.

Colloquy One, 1991. Later, Colloquy Two was made for Ssang Yong Cement in Singapore.
However, the later version had only three figures – 'four' and 'death' being the same word in Chinese!

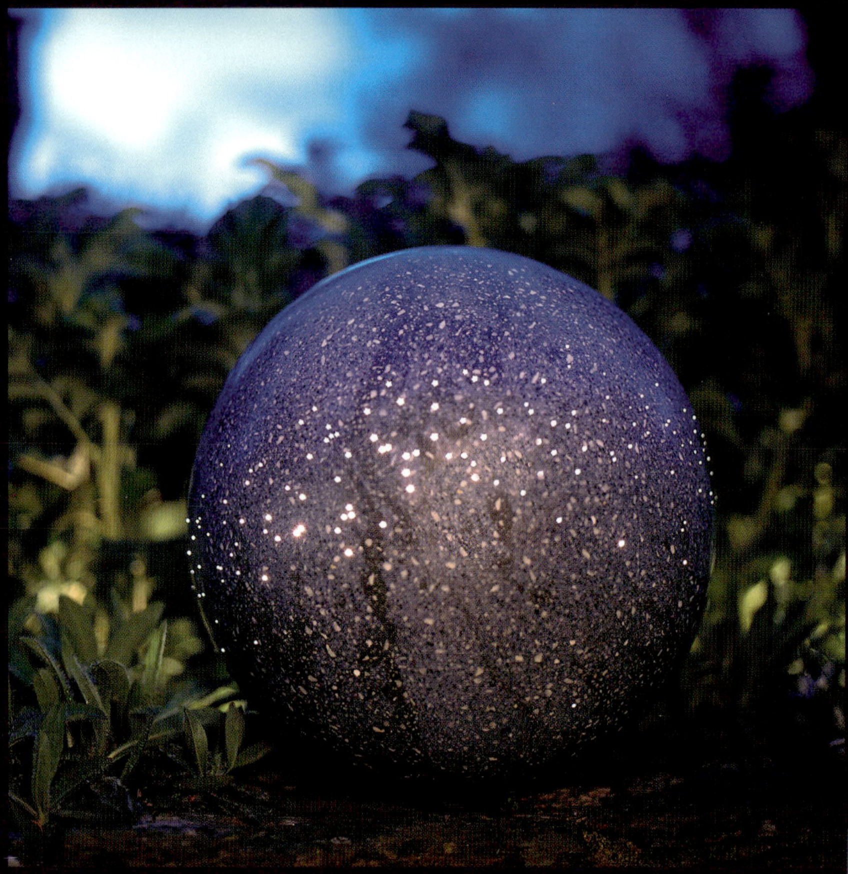

An 18in concrete sphere with fibre-optic lighting by Anthony Fanshawe – the technique was later used in The Bude Light.

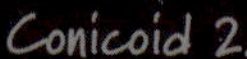

Conicoid 2.

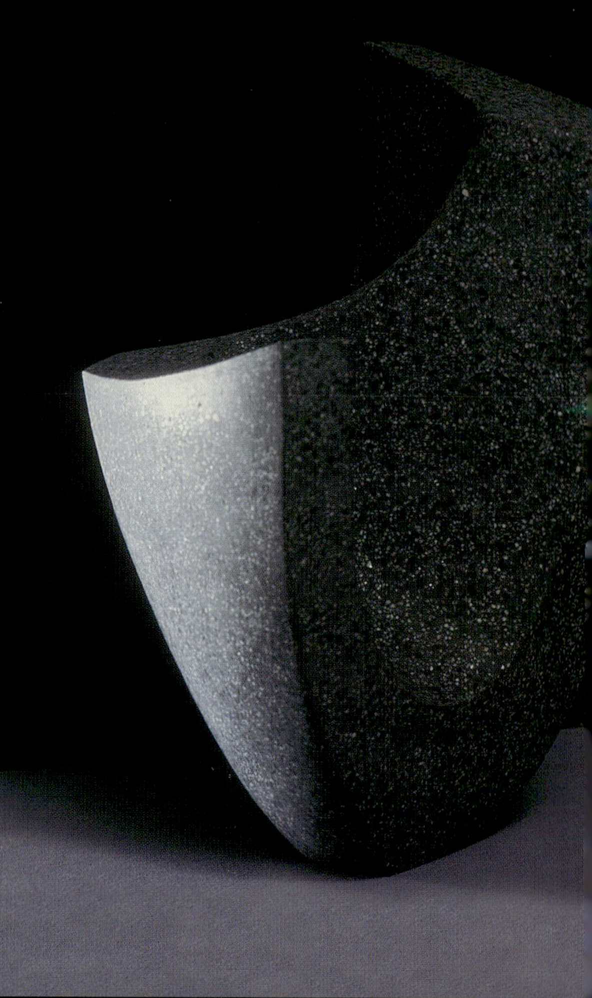

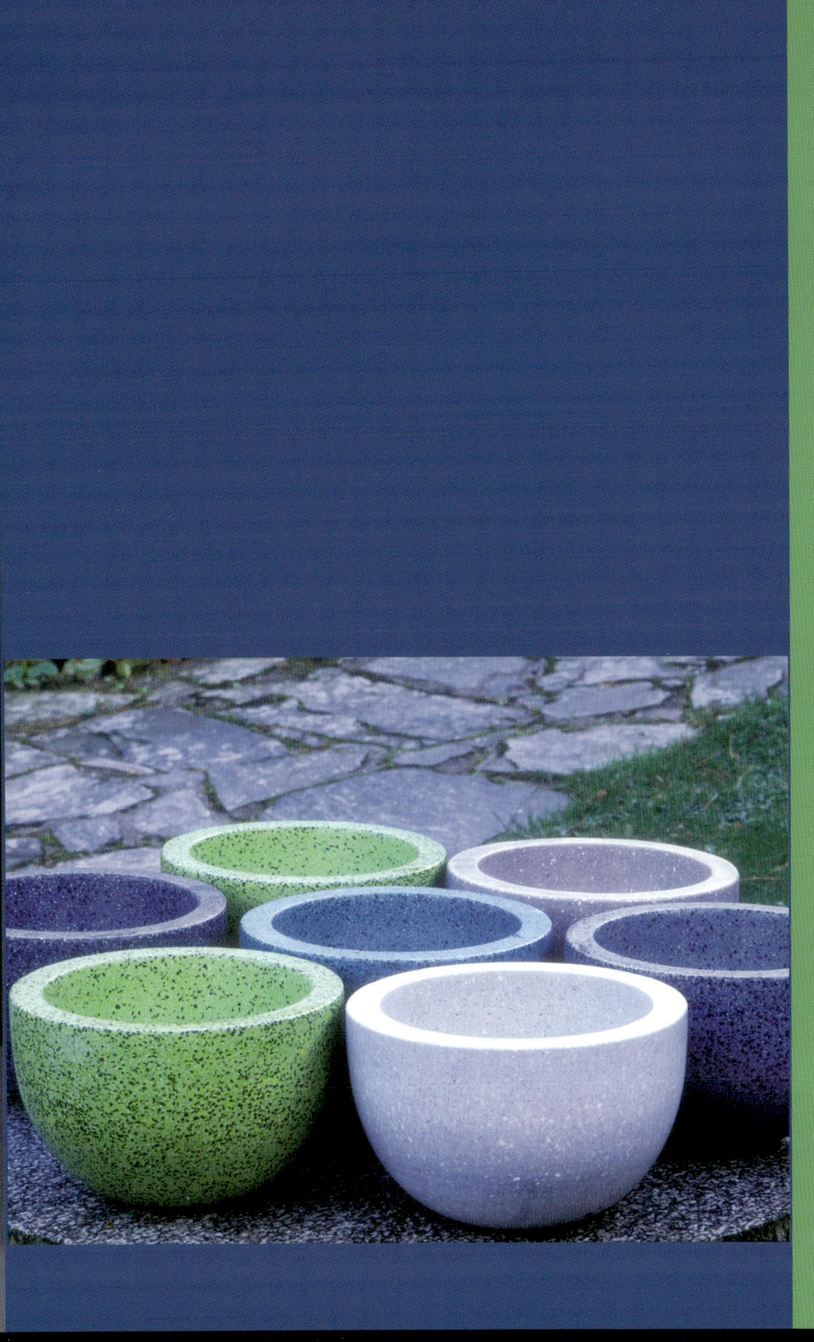

Commissions and public work

1982 **Reunion**
Commission: Miss A.M. Shaw

1984 **One and All**
Commission: W.E. Chivers Ltd., for Old Vicarage Place, St Austell, Cornwall

1985 **The Family**
Location: The Surgery, Boscastle, Cornwall

1988 **The Armada Dial**
Commission: Plymouth City Council, for the city centre

1989 **The Devon Pedestrians**
Commission: Devon County Council, for Exeter, Plymouth, Torquay and Barnstaple

1990–91 **Quartet**
Commission: Marina Rainey for Oldhay, Launceston, Cornwall, and InterCity for The Royal Scottish Academy of Music & Drama

1993 **The Peacock Bowl** at Chelsea Flower Show

1993 **The Buskers**
Commission: Safeway Stores, for Cage Yard, Reigate, Surrey

1994 **Colloquy Two**
Commission: Ssang Yong Cement Ltd., for their offices in Singapore

1995 **Colloquy Two 3/5** for David Bows

1996 **Les Jongleurs**
Commission: Jersey Public Sculpture Trust, St Helier, Jersey

1997 **Atlantis**
Commission: private client, Jersey

1998–9 **The Red Carpet**
Commission: The Edinburgh Festival Society, for The Hub, Highland Tolbooth

2000 **The Bude Light 2000**
Commission: Bude-Stratton Town Council, for The Castle, Bude, Cornwall

2001 **The Blue Circle Garden**
Sponsor: Blue Circle Industries plc.
Location: RHS Chelsea Flower Show

2003–4 **Concrete Jungle**
Proposal for RHS Chelsea Flower Show

acknowledgements

Photographs are by Clive Boursnell, except for the following: Christopher Laughton, pp. 1, 22, 23; Antonia Reeve Photography, p. 35; Donata de Reus, p. 45. Archival photographs by Carole Vincent, Muriel and Bill Blackett, and John Beswick.

First published in 2003 by **Alison Hodge**
Bosulval, Newmill, Penzance, Cornwall TR20 8XA
info@alison-hodge.co.uk
www.alison-hodge.co.uk

Designed by **Christopher Laughton**.

ISBN 0 906720 63 X

A catalogue record for this book is available from the British Library.

Originated by BDP – Book Development and Production, Penzance, Cornwall.

Cover: Half Acre, Concrete Garden

Printed and bound in Spain.